The Hollywood Ripper : The True Story of Michael Gargiulo

Edward Hutton

Published by Trellis Publishing, 2021.

While every precaution has been taken in the preparation of this book, the publisher assumes no responsibility for errors or omissions, or for damages resulting from the use of the information contained herein.

THE HOLLYWOOD RIPPER : THE TRUE STORY OF MICHAEL GARGIULO

First edition. July 5, 2021.

Copyright © 2021 Edward Hutton.

ISBN: 979-8224239733

Written by Edward Hutton.

THE HOLLYWOOD RIPPER

THE TRUE STORY OF MICHAEL GARGIULO
EDWARD HUTTON

Michael Gargiulo, a reasonably good looking man in his mid-40s, sits calmly staring forward listening intently to the back and forth debate that is taking place in front of him. His newly shaven head glistening slightly as cameras click incessantly in the courtroom, trying to capture the face of evil masquerading underneath his handsome mask. With three known murders under his belt; one attempted murder and, it would seem, even from his own very words, potentially more victims out there, getting to understand how Michael Gargiulo could have avoided arrest for some twenty years, beggars' belief.

Born February 15th, 1976 in the quaint suburb of Glenview, Illinois some fifteen miles from Chicago, Michael, together with his brothers and parents, were your typical and average American middle class family. Michael grew up what seemed to be unnoticeable oblivion, attending Glenbrook South High School where his grades remained as unremarkable as did his baseball playing career.

Neighbors, teachers and people who knew of him, now remember how distant and somewhat anti-social Michael had been during his teen years. An individual with a quick temper, Michael never seemed to fit in and seemed to be at odds most of the time with his own existence. He did not communicate well; averaged at school and was characteristic of what we now would often associate with the perfect serial killer – he kept to himself; was a true loner and, aggressive.

Neighbors of course, mention how he often felt uncomfortable hanging around other people and even in other people's houses; almost instantly scratching at the doors to get out like some kind of feral animal.

It was only when 26 year old Michelle Murphy from Santa Monica, managed to fight off a knife-wielding intruder during the early hours of the morning of 28 April 2008, that the truth of Michael's dark nature and his past, began to catch up with him..

Michael's story of psycho-sexual thrill killing – as the prosecutor would eventually describe him, began some twenty years earlier, when as a young teenager, he tasted his first control of life and death to the expense of a young and vibrant Tricia Pacaccio.

Eighteen years old and one year older than Michael at the time, Patricia was a bubbly well liked young woman who also lived in the pretty suburb of Glenview, Illinois. She stayed a mere block away from the Gargiulo family and was well on her way to a bright and rewarding future. She was part of the school debate team, popular with lots of friends and had recently obtained a scholarship to Purdue University. Her future was bright and her positive outlook was set.

She knew Michael. Her younger brother Doug was friends with him and, he had been around to their house on a few occasions. So around 1am on the morning of August 14th 1993, after attending a school rally with friends, she may not have been all that surprised to find him outside her home waiting in the dark. What she didn't realize at the time was that he was waiting for her.

What took place in those brief few seconds or minute before her life ended so abruptly, only Michael himself knows. But now she lay viciously bludgeoned to death on her porch having suffered a dozen or so frenzied knife wounds to her body and face. There was no noise made. No scream - just a swift and evil calculated murder. If she had managed to scream – even just once, her parents would have no doubt, woken, or neighbors would have been quickly alerted and Michael would most likely have fled the scene before finishing his cruel deed. In fact, that very evening, neighbors of the Pocaccio family had hosted a pool party earlier in that quiet cul de sac, but heard and saw nothing. The silence surrounding her painful death continued until her father made the exceptionally grim and horrific discovery of his own daughter's limp body as he stepped out the next morning to collect his paper.

In a small and quiet neighborhood where not much ever happened, this horrific murder had shocked everyone to the core. A rare case of murder and, in such a brutal way, was unheard of. Dozens of people, neighbors and friends were interviewed; leads were followed; suspects drilled on their whereabouts and all alibis supposedly checked, including Michael who denied any involvement. Michael in fact had managed to turn local detective's attention away from himself and onto a friend of his, Erik. What made the whole case so difficult to put together for local detectives, was that there had been no clear motive for such a savage attack on this poor victim – no sexual assault; no robbery; no vendetta to be delivered; just a senseless and repeated frenzied stabbing inflicted on a beautiful, innocent young woman.

Over some ten years, various Illinois detectives from the local sheriff department tried – possibly half-heartedly as time went on – to solve the murder - each of them in turn, taking up the dusty file and revisiting witness statements and potential suspects or motives. Despite DNA evidence of blood and skin fragments found under Tricia's fingernails at the time, suspicions and rumors swirling around in the community and potential flimsy alibis of no substance, Glenview detectives never came close to solving this heinous act of violence. Possibly DNA was not seen as too reliable back then in 1993 but, thankfully someone was fortuitous enough to carefully preserve it for any future leads or suspects who may be found.

Whatever the unfathomable reason is for not solving her murder, Tricia Pocaccio became just another statistical cold case file. And, because her killer was not brought to justice, 3 more innocent victims – that we know of - would have to pay the price before Michael was eventually put behind bars. Tricia's attempt to fend off her attacker, taking those critical particles of his DNA, would become the key some 20 years later to linking Michael Gargiulo to the murder of two further young women and attempted murder of a third. But for Tricia, justice would still have to wait – she still waits today to tell her story of what happened to her on her quiet Glenville porch.

By 1998 some five years after the murder of Tricia Pocaccio, Michael had moved with his brother across country to Los Angeles,

Hollywood where he took up various jobs. In 1999 he held down some odd jobs as a repair man and even a bouncer at the well-known Rainbow Bar & Grill on Sunset Boulevard, before unceremoniously being fired for punching a customer. That same year Michael landed a small acting role playing the part of a boxer in a student's graduate thesis film. This thesis film was written and directed by the now famous LA Movie Producer, Temple Brown., who later commented how perfect Michael Gargiulo had been for his part and that he looked every bit the determined boxer, playing his role well. Even though Michael never become a professional actor or for that matter a professional boxer, his acting skills sure would help him avoid being caught for years to come.

If you thought Michael was potentially inept at relationships, you would be forgiven, but sorely mistaken. A string of girlfriends, casual sexual partners and, secret lovers came in - and quickly out, of his life over the years leading up to his eventual arrest in 2008. In fact by 2008, he was married and had prior to that, fathered two children by two different women.

When Michael moved from Illinois to Los Angeles, his then girlfriend, Alison, later joined him and they both set up home in Orchid Avenue just behind the well-known Grauman's Chinese Theatre in Hollywood. This address was of course, not far from the bungalow of what would become his second victim, Ashley Ellerin.

Ashley Ellerin had just got out of her shower in her quaint home in Hollywood, readying herself for her date with the then unknown actor, Ashton Kutcher. He had called for the second time to update her on his feeble reasons for being late. She was not too fussed as she herself, was not ready yet for their evening out to the watch the Grammys at a friend's place.

It was 8.45pm when she ended her call with Kutcher.

Her hairdryer sat ready on the toilet seat in the bathroom and her curling tongs heating next to the basin.

That morning had been a busy and reasonably fun day for Ellerin and her father who was visiting her and stayed at the Bay Area suburb of Los Altos at the time. They had been working on Ashley's home, doing a bit of painting and remodeling. By late afternoon, she had dropped her father back at the airport and headed back home to meet up with her landlord, Mark Durbin who popped round to help her move some furniture and fix the ceiling fan. She liked him and with whom she had also had a casual on off sexual relationship.

Minutes, maybe only seconds after she hung up the call with Kutcher, dripping wet, her life was brutally and savagely ended with 47 frenzied knife wounds inflicted. She lay dead just outside the bathroom door. Her life and her future cut short at the tender age of 22.

When Kutcher was interviewed by detectives following the gruesome murder he confirmed that Ellerin's lights were on and her car was in the driveway, when he arrived late that night. He got to the property and, since she had not answered his previous two calls – one around 9.30pm and the last when he was driving over eventually at 10.45pm, he thought she was just upset with him for being late. He got out of his car and knocked on the door. No answer. He tried the door handle but it was locked. He peered into the window and saw what looked like some spilled red wine on the floor. She must be angry with me he thought. He left, none the wiser that she was dead just meters from him. If maybe he had picked her up on the evening of 21st February 2001 at the time they had initially agreed which was to have been around 8.30pm, she may not have died that night. But she did – and savagely so.

How did Michael and Ashley's path cross? By fate – as I am sure, most murderers would prefer to say. Around October of 2000, Ashley Ellerin stood outside her yellow bungalow smiling in amusement while she watched her friend Christopher Duran attempt to fix his flat tire. Like prince charming, a handsome savior came walking over and offered his help. It was Michael Gargiulo. Of course, Michael's attention was drawn to the beautiful blonde and petite bombshell that stood by her friend with a big warm and friendly smile. Ashley was indeed a beautiful young woman who had found it easy to attract boyfriends and potential dates and was a young and vivacious student from the L.A. Fashion Institute of Design and Merchandising. Ashely had also recently and briefly dated some soon-to-be well known Hollywood Actors, including Vin Diesel, Jeremy Sisto, her then landlord, Christopher Durin and of course, Ashton Kutcher.

Michael helped and introduced himself as a local air-conditioning repairman, giving the pair his card and chatting with them. After all, it was a happy coincidence that he lived nearby with his girlfriend in the Armor Arms on Orchid Avenue.

Over the coming months, Michael became a regular – maybe too regular a visitor to Ashely and then roommate, Justin Peterson's home.

Looking back, it is chilling to hear the fresh testimonies from Ellerin's friends and associates. All of them had thought Michael a strange and obsessive character, explaining how he would constantly stare at Ashley or park outside her home in the early hours of the morning in his green pick-up truck. Yes, Michael had even been confronted by Ashley's roommate on one of these occasions. The excuse given by Michael at the time would have sent most of us running to the police. He told Patterson that he had been linked to a murder near Chicago, that police and FBI were showing up, and that they were after a DNA sample from him. Peterson also later testified that Gargiulo had shown him a hunting knife strapped to his ankle. As if that wasn't enough to seriously question Michael's intent, one of Michael's numerous secret lovers, Velma Carillo, also testified how Michael had told her he had left Illinois because of a murder he didn't commit but that his DNA had been found at the scene.

This trend of chilling stories and tales Michael apparently told many of the people he met, went unnoticed – like the boy who cried wolf maybe. They heard his strange tales; saw his hunting knife strapped to his ankle; watched him stalk a friend; even listened to him admit to murdering someone in Chicago years earlier – and did nothing.

Naivety does not come close to describing the lacking insight of those around not only Ashley, but more importantly Michael. Ashley may herself have been naïve, surrounded by the lights and glam of a partying Hollywood, but who befriends an individual who boasts blatantly of such a dark past?

Despite all the warning signs and suspicions, on the evening of 21 February 2001, Ashley lay dead on the wet floor of her bathroom; brutally and savagely stabbed to death.

What happened in Michael's life between 2001 and 2005 or who he met remains somewhat unclear, if not undocumented. What was clear however, was that he was nowhere in the frame at the time for this second murder. Detectives on the case had questioned and ruled out numerous suspects and could not track down someone called "Mike the furnace man" who Ashley's friends had mentioned but knew little about. Michael who had visited Ashely's home uninvited several times and who had attended a few parties; who had told countless strange and dark tales of his past, was essentially, anonymous. Detective Small, who was on the case even managed to track down a 'Michael' who had been involved in an accident, knocking down a dog on Orchard Avenue in 2002. He showed Michael's picture to Ashley's friends who recognized him.

This yet insignificant lead was the start of two things – Michael's eventual capture but also, as the result of the most blatant ineffectual police work, the death of Gargiulo's third official victim and attempted murder of his fourth.

As it happened, in 2002, detectives from Illinois, following up the murder of Tricia Pocaccio in 1993, made their way to Lost Angeles to acquire a DNA sample from none other than Michael Garguilo. They had made contact with Detective Small's team in order to get their assistance in tracking down Michael. This was at the same time that Small was trying to track down Michael in connection with the death of Ashley Ellerin.

Detective Small had only just discovered the identity of the person responsible for the dog accident on Orchard Avenue – the same Michael Gargiulo. As if fate itself was screaming from the heavens, the two detective teams from Los Angeles and Glenview came together and compared notes on the two brutal killings that had taken place close to a decade apart and on opposite sides of the country. The similarities were astounding.

Wasting no time, detectives tracked down Gargiulo who was now living in West Los Angeles with his new girlfriend, Grace Kwak who he had also met online through the dating website, Match.com. Forcefully taking a blood sample from their suspect in December 2002, detectives were now certain they had found their man.

If you thought DNA would take a mere few weeks, at best, to come back from the labs, again you would be sorely mistaken. It took until September 2003, some ten months later, for the results to match up to the DNA found under Tricia Pocaccio fingernails.

This should have been the end to Michael's violent murderous rampage. But Maria Bruno would still die in 2005 and Michelle Murphy would still almost die in 2008.

What can only be described as one of the most inept and bungling piece of police work to date, Cook County prosecutors declined to file charges against Michael Gargiulo citing the evidence strong enough to make a case against the suspect and that, potentially the DNA under Tricia's fingernails had found its way there quite innocently.

So, if you are looking for who was responsible for the death of Gargiulo's next victim, Maria Bruno, look no further than the decisions made by both the then State's Attorney, Richard A. Devine, and his side-kick Special Prosecutor, Scott Cassidy who both declined to pursue the evidence.

This blatant disregard for evidence also had a knock on effect to the murder of Ashley Ellerin. No longer could Detective Small or the LAPD arrest Gargiulo for her murder since they themselves had found no human trace evidence at the crime scene that could link directly back to Michael Gargiulo.

Michael was free to continue with his warped and sadistic inner demons. By September 2005, Michael and a now pregnant Grace Kwak moved into a gated second floor apartment on Arden Way in El Monte, East Los Angeles. The relationship between the two was characteristic of most of Michael's relationships – rocky, abusive and quickly over.

Thanksgiving weekend was around the corner and soon, just a few days later, 32-year-old Maria Bruno would excitedly move into her unit on the first floor of this same gated complex.

Maria was a remarkably beautiful young mother of four who had just taken up a position as a clerk at a local furniture store in El Monte. Of El Salvadoran decent, she had recently separated from her husband and was now trying to start her new life.

But on December 01st, 2005, just ten days after she had moved into her place on Arden way, she lay slaughtered on her new apartment floor, stabbed seventeen times; her throat slashed and her chest mutilated. It was her estranged husband who discovered her body; thankfully not her children.

Again, as if by fate, neighbors were interviewed and witnesses who had seen someone trying to enter Maria's apartment a few days earlier, saw nothing, did nothing and said nothing. No one in this secured gated community fell under suspicion and no criminal records existed for anyone who lived near Maria. Knocking on Gargiulo's door several times and leaving their card after no answer, still did not make the police any the wiser as to the sadistic criminal that lived just meters from this unfortunate victim.

Pregnant girlfriend, Grace Kwak had moved back to her parents to get away from her abusive boyfriend, just prior to Maria's murder. She did however, come across a police flyer some time later that had been pasted to a restaurant bathroom wall and detailed the murder. Her face turning pale, she realized the victim stay in the same gate community and address as where she and Michael lived. In her concern, she made contact with Michael, who, she testified, 'revealed he knew the victim, helped her carry her groceries and had even said she was beautiful.'

Maria Bruno's murder remained unsolved and no DNA evidence could be linked to any potential suspect.

2005 came and went. So did 2006, 2007 and, by 2008, Gargiulo had married and was living with his new wife and mother in her Santa Monica apartment on Euclid Avenue.

Target number four was Michelle Murphy, a bubbling and enthusiastic 26 year old young woman who, on the evening of April 28th, 2008, climbed into bed and readied herself for a peaceful night.

Michelle also stayed on Euclid Avenue. In fact, she lived in her second floor apartment just across the alley way from Michael Gargiulo and his wife. That day she busied herself with those mundane house chores we all hate to do and finishing up with her laundry. Michelle had then gone into the alley way to do her exercise routine of skipping rope and sprints, before showering, eating and watching a last bit of TV and heading to bed.

She was suddenly and horrifically woken to a man looming over her, stabbing her repeatedly. She fought, screaming and physically kicked her attacker for the sake of her life. If she hadn't, she would have been official victim number 4.

The attacker had managed to somehow pry open a window and was not hovering over her wielding and stabbing his serrated knife several times into her arm, chest and hand. How this petite 5ft 1nch brunette managed to hold off her attacker enough to survive is remarkable in itself. But, grabbing for the knife held tightly in his hand, Michelle Murphy managed to push the blade back, cutting Michael's own hand in the process. Michelle brought up her legs and kicked at him, pushing him off her.

As Gargiulo fell backward and off the bed, it was as if he had just been snapped out of some kind of thrill seeking catatonic state. He clambered down her hallway away from the bedroom and yelped a strange 'I'm sorry' before escaping through the front door of the apartment. Michelle, sobbing, wounded and bleeding profusely, quickly locked her front door before dialing her boyfriend and 911.

The path to Michael Gargiulo's arrest had eventually found a clearing in this mad forest of insanity. DNA evidence – hard blood evidence of Michelle Murphy's attacker, now lay waiting to be discovered on her bedspread.

Sergeant Lewis of the Santa Monica Police Department was lead on the Michelle Murphy case and ordered the attacker's blood sample left behind, be tested for potential DNA matches in all police databases. Four weeks later, a DNA hit came back. It was the DNA swab that had been taken from Michael Gargiulo by police investigating potential suspects to the murders of Tricia Pacaccio of Glenview, Illinois and Ashley Ellerin from Hollywood, California.

It was the same lead Sergeant of Michelle's attempted murder case who recalled a conversation he had with Los Angeles detectives just some months earlier regarding the slaying of Maria Bruno.

The cases began to mold together, showing a painful and unfortunate story of missed opportunities and incomplete, if not incompetent police work. Different women of different ages from different counties and suburbs, now all found to have been killed by the same serial killer.

Michael Gargiulo was arrested on June 6, 2008, initially by the Santa Monica Police Department and charged with the attempted murder of Michelle Murphy. It was only later on during his incarceration that the further murders of Ashley Ellerin and Maria Bruno were added to the list.

For Tricia Pocaccio, Michael Gargiulo's first victim twenty years earlier, there is now some light shed into the darkness that has surrounded her family's fight for justice.

Had Tricia's family and indeed, the Cook County Sheriff Department, been successful earlier; friends and family listened to earlier; had the police followed up the DNA evidence found under Tricia's fingernails with just that little more of an effort; had associates and family members of Michael come forward earlier with their suspicions; then maybe, just maybe Ashley Ellerin would be married to Ashton Kutcher by now and Maria Bruno would be celebrating yet another happy birthday with one of her children.

Twenty years on, we can at least say that the truth has shone through – the truth always comes out as they say. Better late than never they say. I would rather it was better earlier, than later – at least I am sure both Ashley and Maria would have prayed this was the case.

Michael Garguilo is currently on trial for the murders of Ashley Ellerin in 2001, Maria Bruno in 2005 and the attempted murder of Michelle Murphy in 2008. Illinois criminal proceedings will hopefully follow suit so that Tricia too, may rest in peace.

THE TRAILSIDE KILLER
TERI DAVIDSON

David Carpenter ("Trailside Killer")

David Carpenter, also known as the Trailside Killer, stalked, sexually assaulted, and murdered mostly women on hiking trails near San Francisco, California, with a few victims in Santa Cruz, California. Most of his victims were shot in the head, execution-style, while a couple of them were stabbed to death. Carpenter's reign of terror lasted from 1979 into 1981 when he was subsequently arrested, tried, and convicted of death.

One of his victims, Stephen Haertle, survived being shot multiple times by Carpenter—even though his girlfriend Ellen Hansen was killed—and was able to give police a description of his assailant. Additional witness testimony placed a small red foreign car in the area. Carpenter matched the composite drawn from Haertle's description and he also owned a car that matched the description of the one on the scene at the time of Hansen's and Haertle's attack.

Carpenter was convicted in two separate trials; one in Los Angeles and one in San Diego. Both trials were relocated due to defense attorneys' requests for changes of venue.

He was ultimately sentenced to death and is currently on San Quentin's death row. Carpenter is 85 years of age.

Early Life

David Joseph Carpenter was born on 6 May 1930 in San Francisco—a place that would later become his hunting grounds. As a child, he was physically abused and neglected by his alcoholic father while his near-blind mother was overly domineering. By the time he was seven years old, his stutter was so bad that he couldn't function in any social situation. Many experts assert that his stuttering was likely a result of stress, self-perceived inadequacy, and not feeling safe as a child.

Consequently he was ridiculed which made him overly reclusive. Instead of therapy he was forced to take ballet and piano lessons.

To relieve his frustrations, Carpenter suffered from a bedwetting problem and also tortured animals; thus fulfilling two of the three prongs of the classic serial killer triad, with the other being a preoccupation with setting fires.

From a young age he also had an insatiable sex drive and would look for opportunities to express this. At the age of 17 Carpenter was incarcerated for molesting two of his young cousins. He served a year in the custody of the California Youth Authority and apparently learned nothing because after his release he was even more predatory; offending until he got married in 1955.

Carpenter worked a number of jobs, including as a cruise ship's purser, a salesman, and a printer.

Carpenter and his wife had three children and Carpenter's demanding libido got to be too much for her. Eventually his wife was not enough to satisfy him. In addition to his violent rages he would prowl around, looking for other women. When his drive became so desperate, he resorted to violence.

By serial killer standards, Carpenter was a late bloomer. His first serious violent offense occurred in 1960 when he was arrested and incarcerated for attempted murder for attacking a woman with a hammer and knife. He had befriended this woman and invited her over to meet his wife and family. One day he picked her up for work but instead of driving her there he drove to a wooded area near the Presidio and then pretended to be lost. At some point he grabbed her, straddled her, and tied her up with a clothesline. He then threatened her with a knife, forcing her to be still and telling her that he had a "funny quirk" that needed to be satisfied. When she resisted he struck her multiple times with a hammer. Her cries for help alerted a nearby military patrol officer who, essentially, saved her life. When commanded to stop, Carpenter shot at the officer and was met with return gunfire which wounded Carpenter. He was then arrested. The victim survived. The victim described his speech to investigators as slow and deliberate, thus suggesting that when Carpenter feels as though he is in charge of a situation and asserting himself then he loses his stutter.

While initially sentenced to 14 years, Carpenter served just nine before being released in 1969. Tired of his sexual demands and temper—and having just given birth to their third child—his wife divorced him. When questioned about what caused the divorce Carpenter's story would change, thus indicating that he learned to tell people what he thought they wanted to hear.

Carpenter was remarried quickly after his release and in less than a year this marriage failed as he was back to his old tricks. He once tried to rape a woman by hitting her car to force her out of it. As she struggled with him he stabbed her but she managed to get back into her car and get help.

At this point there is little doubt that Carpenter wanted to rape again but not return to prison so he was prepared to eliminate any witnesses.

He was rearrested on 3 February 1970, in Modesto, California, on kidnapping and robbery charges. Before being transferred to prison, however, he and four other inmates escaped from the Calaveras County Jail. After recapture by the Federal Bureau of Investigation, Carpenter was incarcerated for seven years on the kidnapping and robbery charges, with two more for violating parole. He served his time and was then paroled in May 1979, without being listed as a sex offender which he should have been. In August of that year he murdered his first of many victims.

Carpenter found a job at a photo print shop in San Francisco after he left prison and by all measures appeared to be on the right path to becoming a productive and law-abiding citizen.

The Crimes

Edda Kane

44-year-old married bank executive Edda Kane disappeared from Mount Tamalpais Park near San Francisco Bay on 19 August 1979, while hiking in the part of the park nicknamed "the Sleeping Lady" to revel in the glorious view of the Golden Gate Bridge. As she enjoyed an athletic lifestyle and could not find someone to accompany her on her hike that day, she decided to go out alone. When she did not return home that day her husband called the police who sent out a search team with dogs in case she had fallen and required assistance.

Kane's vehicle was in the parking lot where she left it but there were no signs of the missing woman.

She was later found off Rock Spring Trail on 20 August 1979, naked and shot to death. Forensic experts surmised that she had been attacked from behind and then shot execution-style with a bullet in the back of the head based upon the position of her body on its knees with her face in the dirt. $10 was missing from her wallet, along with some credit cards. The attacker took her glasses but left her jewelry.

This was the first murder on Mount Tamalpais.

Kane's autopsy demonstrated that she had been shot once in the back of the head with a .44 caliber gun. As she had not been raped, police were dumbfounded as to the motive for the attack. Nobody who knew the victim could think of anyone who would want to do her any harm and the lack of evidence did not permit police to fully investigate her death. After a short time her murder became an unsolved isolated homicide and things returned to normal until the following spring.

Barbara Schwartz

On 7 March 1980, 23-year-old baker Barbara Schwartz had gone hiking in Mount Tamalpais State Park with her dog and had never returned.

She was found on a narrow unpaved trail, stabbed to death in the chest. A witness who had watched the entire crime ran for help and, thus, led the rangers to the crime scene. The witness was hiking in the area when she saw through the trees a thin, athletic man, about 25 years of age approach Schwartz whose dog was barking. She said the assailant "had a hawk nose and dark hair, and he wore hiking boots." The witness then stated that the man and victim struggled for nearly a minute and then he left as Schwartz fell to the ground which was when she left to seek help. Unfortunately, the witness' description of the assailant was "wildly erroneous in every respect" and she, in fact, later admitted this herself. Consequently, investigators were misled, thus delaying the search for the actual culprit.

Other witnesses said they had seen a lone male in his 40s, wearing glasses, and clad in a raincoat despite the fact that it wasn't raining that day. This man was most likely Schwartz's killer.

The bifocals found near Schwartz's body turned out to be prison-issued so investigators began to look at recently-released convicts, particularly those with a record of sex crimes who bore some resemblance to the witness description of the assailant. The San Francisco office of the FBI assisted with the investigation but to no avail.

Interestingly, however, police in another jurisdiction did question a man who claimed to have been wounded in a convenience store attack; however, these officers did not have access to the Marin County all-points bulletin and, therefore, were unable to make a possible connection that this quiet man may have been responsible for Schwartz's murder. The next day the same wounded man visited an optometrist—Schwartz's doctor, in fact—to get a new pair of glasses. The previous day the police had questioned the doctor about Schwartz's prescription; however, he had no knowledge of the eyeglasses found at the scene of the crime. If he had then he might have recognized the "unique prescription" his new patient had.

During Schwartz's autopsy, the pathologist counted 12 separate stab wounds in her chest, likely made with a ten-inch knife. Several days later, some kids found a blood-crusted boning knife near the crime scene which was determined to have been purchased at a large chain grocery store. A television reporter had subsequently handled the knife, thus obliterating any fingerprints which might have been left by the murderer. Forensic evidence suggested that she, too, had been in a kneeling position when she died.

Anne Alderson

On 15 October 1980, 26-year-old former Peace Corps volunteer Anne Alderson entered the park to go for a jog and to demonstrate that the park was, for the most part, safe. Many witnesses saw her and the park's caretaker even remembered her sitting alone in the 5,000-seat amphitheater to watch the sunset. Earlier that day some of the same witnesses reported seeing a lone male around 50 years of age in the park "just standing around."

She was found the next day with a .38 caliber bullet in her head. This crime scene was different from the others in that Alderson was raped, then permitted to get dressed before being murdered. She was found propped, face up, against a rock with her right earring missing. Investigators believed that "her twisted arrangement" indicated that she may have been forced to kneel as well before being shot.

Mark McDermand—A Red Herring

Police thought they had the person responsible for her death when they investigated a double homicide on 16 October 1980, near Mount Tamalpais in Mill Valley. Mark McDermand, 35, and his brother, Edwin, 40, both lived with their mother, Helen, 75. At approximately 8:30 p.m. deputies responded to a call by a concerned friend. After forcing their way into the home, deputies found the body of a man lying in a hallway who was identified as Edwin. He had been shot in the head and chest. In a locked bedroom deputies found the deceased body of Helen, lying on the bed and covered by a blanket. She had a single bullet hole behind her left ear. Eight spent .22 caliber casings were found near the bodies.

Deputies found a small padlocked door that led to the basement. They discovered a note tacked to the inside of the door addressed to "Shitheels" that said that by the time the note and bodies were discovered it would be "way too late" and that the perpetrator would be found either "on the news or on a 'slab'". The note was signed "Mr. Hate."

Inside the room were spent .38 caliber casings, three .22 caliber bullets, and ankle holsters for a pistol and a knife. This smelly basement room had been Mark McDermand's bedroom and became the prime suspect.

The coroner said that the bodies had been dead for three or four days.

A few days later, the local newspaper and the Marin County Sheriff's Department received letters from an individual claiming responsibility for the double homicide and a handwriting expert stated that the same person who wrote the note at the McDermand's house also wrote these letters. In these letters, the writer stated that he would not be captured alive so on 24 October detectives devised a plan to lure him by running an ad directed at him with a phone number that said that if he surrendered he would be treated fairly.

McDermand called the number that evening and said that he was considering surrendering but that "he had some things to do first." He called again two days later with details about the murders; saying that he tried to kill his mother and brother quickly but miscalculated with Edwin, hence the multiple gunshot wounds. He said that he had to "stop Edwin from hurting others" and that he would turn himself in the next day.

When McDermand approached the police he was wearing a belt with a .38 caliber revolver and also had a set of thumb cuffs and three speed loaders. In his vehicle was a 12-gauge shotgun, a .22 caliber pistol, ammunition, a metal box containing several hypodermic syringes, and some insulin as McDermand was diabetic.

He told police that his brother was schizophrenic and had been deteriorating quickly so he borrowed the guns and then prepared to go on the run after the deed was done. McDermand said that he acted out of diminished capacity and that he, too, was schizophrenic and couldn't remember the murders or when he did he told several different stories.

Nevertheless, the jury found McDermand guilty of two counts of first-degree murder and he received the death penalty.

At the end of it all, investigators resolved his potential part in the trailside murders as none of his firearms matched the bullets found in the victims on Mount Tampalpais. That and the fact that the murders continued.

Shauna May

On 27 November 1980 25-year-old Shauna May disappeared from Point Reyes National Seashore Park while hiking. She was supposed to meet friends the following day to do more hiking. They had selected this area because it was several miles north of San Francisco and had not had the dubious distinction of having had a murder occur there recently. When she failed to show up, her friends alerted park officials.

Two days later her body was found by hikers who had seen her foot protruding from a shallow grave. She had been strangled with picture frame wire, shot three times in the head, and shoved into a shallow trench. She had also been raped.

Her body was found in close proximity to Diane O'Connell.

Diane O'Connell

The body of 22-year-old Diane O'Connell was found the same day and near May's body. She had disappeared a month earlier from the same area while hiking with friends as well and her body was rather decomposed. She had been raped, strangled with wire, and shot once in the head.

It was initially believed that the two women perhaps knew each other and were killed at around the same time as another hiker reported hearing four gunshots in that area of the park during the mid-afternoon.

The two women were laying together, face down. Their collective clothing was piled atop a backpack. A pair of underwear was stuffed into O'Connell's mouth. After investigating, it was determined that the two women did not know each other.

Richard Stowers and Cynthia Moreland

As if finding two bodies wasn't bad enough, police also discovered the bodies of 19-year-old Richard Towers and his girlfriend, 18-year-old Cynthia Moreland on the same day as May's and O'Connell's. The couple had been missing since 11 October, having last been seen by friends who they told that they were going to go hiking in the park. In fact, Stowers was in the Coast Guard and was reported as being AWOL.

Both victims had been murdered execution-style with bullets to the head.

An autopsy placed their time of death mere days before Alderson's, thus suggesting that there were two murderers or that a single killer had gone hunting for victims in two different areas. When ballistics determined that the bullet from Alderson's head matched those in both Stowers and Moreland, authorities knew there was just one single deadly predator.

Visitors were told not to go hiking alone; however, being together did not save Stowers and Moreland. Those who typically frequented the parks stayed away or went elsewhere until the murderer was caught.

Needless to say, the media frenzy that ensued wreaked panic throughout the area.

Was David Carpenter the Elusive Zodiac Killer?

Between December 1968 and July 1969 a man shot two couples on two separate occasions in Vallejo, California and then taunted detectives with phone calls claiming responsibility. One of the victims survived and was able to give police a description. Soon thereafter, editors of three San Francisco newspapers each received part of a strange letter also claiming to be from the killer. His message "consisted of a printed cryptogram composed of symbols and signed with a crossed-circle symbol" and all three of the letters had to be put together to decipher it. A local teacher was able to crack the code which stated that the killer enjoyed killing and it was his intention to continue doing so. He signed his letter "the Zodiac."

On 27 September 1969, while 20-year-old Bryan Hartnell and 22-year-old Cecelia Ann Shepard were picnicking at Lake Berryessa, a man in a black executioner's hood approached them. He stabbed Shepard ten times—five in the front and five in the back—and Hartnell six times in the back. He then called the police to report it.

Two weeks later the killer struck again, killing cab driver Paul Stine. The *San Francisco Chronicle* received a letter soon after accompanied by a torn piece of the shirt Stine was wearing at the time of his death. Investigators developed a number of suspects but none checked out. This serial killer was very clever and turned his escapades into multilayered games before he withdraw and maintained a low profile. This was quite disturbing for investigators who never knew when or where he would resurface.

In 1980, former FBI profiler John Douglas—who had been on the Zodiac case since it began—assisted sex crimes expert Special Agent Roy Hazelwood and San Francisco police to help create a profile of the Trailside Killer.

After examining the crime scene data and photos, Douglas concluded that the killer would be a local man who was shy, reclusive, and may have a speech impediment. Douglas also added that the murderer was likely socially awkward, white, intelligent, blue collar, and had spent time incarcerated. He was presumed to choose his victims out of opportunity rather than hunting the same type of victim. His modus operandi (MO) was to approach from behind and overwhelm his victim—"like a spider waiting for a bug to fly into his web." Douglas added that the killer would also have at least two of three specific background indicators common to many serial killers:

bedwetting, fire-starting, and cruelty to animals. Finally, Douglas had said while the suspect likely committed rape in his past he had not killed anyone before his current murderous rampage. When questioned about the very specific speech impediment predictor, Douglas said that the secluded killing areas and method of approach indicated some type of shyness and/or shame and he believed it was due to some physical malady that really bothered the killer. Therefore, he attacked in the way he did to compensate for his handicap. While being very detailed, however, police still didn't have any potential suspects.

After Douglas returned to Quantico the Trailside Killer struck again.

Carpenter was ultimately cleared of any involvement with the Zodiac murders through fingerprint and handwriting analysis.

Ellen Hansen

On 29 March 1981, University of California at Davis undergraduate students Ellen Hansen and her boyfriend Stephen Haertle were ambushed in Henry Cowell State Park near Santa Cruz; another town that experienced a spate of murders during the early 1970s committed by Edmund Kemper, John Linley Frazier, and Herbert Mullin—all of whom were safely incarcerated at that time.

Carpenter approached the couple with a pistol in his hand and threatened the pair, insisting that Hansen permit him to rape her. Of course she refused, telling him off. Carpenter then opened fire, shooting Hansen point blank in the head twice and once in the shoulder. The assailant then shot Haertle and left him for dead. Haertle crawled for help despite wounds that ripped through his neck, a hand, and one eye. He proved instrumental in providing police with a partial description of the murderer: near 50, balding, approximately five-foot-ten to six-feet tall and approximately 170 pounds, with crooked yellow teeth, wearing dark glasses as well as a gold jacket with lettering on the back and a baseball cap. Haertle also remembered that the assailant had spoken in "quick, commanding sentences." This description differed considerably from the description of the Marin County killer; however, the MO was the same.

Other hikers reported that they had seen a man matching the description of the gunman in a red, late model, foreign car, running through the park after the gunshots had been fired.

Investigators were also able to lift some good shoeprint impressions to compare to a suspect when they got one.

Authorities released a composite drawing based upon Haertle's and other witness' descriptions in a number of newspapers to both alert people and hopefully get some leads. Four days later a woman called to describe a man she had met 26 years earlier on a cruise to Japan. She said that the purser on the cruise was a young man named David Carpenter who had been bothering her and her daughter with inappropriate behavior. She also recalled that he stuttered.

Presumably reading the paper and staying abreast with detectives' search for the Trailside Killer, Carpenter decided to grow a beard.

He then decided to kill much closer to home, enabling police to catch him.

Heather Scaggs

On 1 May 1981 police caught a break; however, it would come with another victim. On that day, 20-year-old Heather Scaggs disappeared on her way en route to buy a car with help from a coworker, one David Carpenter; they both worked at Econo Quick Print. She had told her boyfriend, Dan Pingle, that Carpenter "made a special point" of asking her to come alone when she came by to get the car and that his friend was selling it and Carpenter was going to help her purchase it. It was Pingle who informed police that she was missing. Luckily Scaggs had left Carpenter's address and phone number with him.

Scaggs' decomposing body was found on 24 May 1981 in Big Basin Redwood State Park, north of San Francisco. Ballistics from recovered bullets proved that she had been murdered with the same pistol used on Haertle and Hansen. She had also been raped and the DNA from the semen inside of her matched Carpenter.

Anna Menjivas

On 16 June 1981 a jaw bone later identified as belonging to Anna Menjivas was found by rock climbers in Castle Rock State Park. She had been missing since 28 December 1980 and was 17 years old at the time of her disappearance. She had worked part-time at the bank where Carpenter was a client and he often struck up conversation with her. Many believed that he only came into the bank to talk to her. Because the cause of death could not be established and there was scant evidence against him, he was not charged for her murder even though authorities were certain that he had killed her. Her name was added to the list of Carpenter's victims to bring his total to ten murders.

Investigation and Arrest

When police went to Carpenter's house to question him, they couldn't help but notice that Carpenter looked quite like the man in the composite sketch and that he had a shiny red Fiat.

Police discovered that Carpenter had not shown up on any released inmates' records where they initially searched due to a technicality: that he had been released by the state of California to serve a federal sentence and, while out on parole, was technically in federal custody. This issue resulted in the delay and subsequent difficulty in identifying him. That he was a habitual sex offender was another important factor not fully documented in his records.

The police department and FBI set up a surveillance van outside the house at 36 Sussex Street in San Francisco where Carpenter lived with his aging parents and also followed him on his errands, especially when he associated with other known criminals. They approached Carpenter who was walking down the street one day with a shopping bag in his hand to apprehend him. Initially confused, Carpenter then asked for a lawyer; at this point he was told that he was under arrest, to which he, strangely, begged, "Please don't hurt me."

Officers executed a search warrant on Carpenters home and car and found books about local hiking trails and over 60 maps. They talked to Carpenter's former fiancée who told them that he claimed that the gold jacket he once owned was stolen around the time of the Hansen murder; thus circumstantially placing him at the scene where Haertle and Hansen were shot. Further, Carpenter's car matched the one described by the surviving victim and several witnesses, he had the same optometrist as another victim, he had the right distinctive type of clothing, he had a record for violent sex offenses, he suffered from explosive rage and tried to change his appearance with different glasses and facial hair, and he matched many descriptions witnesses gave as the man who had been seen in the area of multiple attacks.

Haertle picked Carpenter's mugshot as the man who shot him and killed his girlfriend. Out of seven more witnesses present at a lineup, six picked him out although not all of them were sure. Police also conducted a car lineup with witnesses identifying Carpenter's Fiat.

He was formally charged with Hansen's murder and Haertle's attempted murder. At his arraignment Carpenter stuttered so badly that he had a difficult time answering the judges questions.

Police were never able to recover the .45 caliber gun that was used in several of his murders; however, a .38 caliber gun that Carpenter had sold to another man, who was on trial for robbery and gladly relinquished it to authorities, was later proven to be the firearm used in the last two murders.

Trial and Conviction

Carpenter's defense attorneys requested a change of venue due to the publicity surrounding his ten murders. However, if attorneys had thought it would make a difference they were mistaken. A change of venue would do nothing to eliminate the incriminating evidence police had against Carpenter. In April 1984, his Los Angeles trial began and on 6 July 1984, Carpenter was convicted of the Santa Cruz murders of Heather Scaggs and Ellen Hansen, and the attempted murder of

Stephen Haertle thanks to the damning evidence that his gun was the one responsible for their deaths. A second jury sentenced Carpenter to die in San Quentin's gas chamber based upon three special circumstances that warranted the death penalty: that he had committed multiple murders; that he had murdered during commission of rape; and that he had lain in wait for his victims. Judge Dion Morrow told the court that, "The defendant's entire life has been a continuous expression of violence and force almost beyond exception. I must conclude with the prosecution that if ever there was a case appropriate for the death penalty, this is it."

Carpenter's second trial began on 5 January 1988 in San Diego. On 10 May 1988, a San Diego jury found Carpenter guilty for five murders. Carpenter was also found guilty of two counts of rape and one count of attempted rape. This trial was different in that Carpenter himself took the stand in his own behalf. He was on the stand for seven days.

Marin County District Attorney Jerry Herman announced that he wouldn't file any charges against Carpenter for Kane's and Schwartz's murders due to inadequate evidence.

In 1994, potential juror misconduct in the second trial was brought to light in that the jury forewoman had known about Carpenter's convictions in Los Angeles for the Santa Cruz murders and had concealed this fact during voir dire for the Marin County trial. Carpenter was not retried as he had already been sentenced to death for other murders. On 6 March 1995 the California Supreme Court refused to give Carpenter a new trial. Justice Armand Arabian said that it was virtually impossible to keep secrets in cases such as this and that he believed that the juror's knowledge had not unduly biased the jury.

In 1997, the California Supreme Court upheld Carpenter's death sentence for the Scaggs and Hansen murders and on 29 November 199 they upheld Carpenter's death penalty from his second trial, with six of the seven justices agreeing that he had a fair trial for the five Marin County murders and had, in fact, been sentenced properly.

In December 2009, San Francisco police reexamined evidence from the 21 October 1979 murder of Mary Frances Bennett. Bennett was 23 years old at the time she was killed. She had been jogging near the Palace of the Legion of Honor in Land's End Park in San Francisco when she was ambushed and stabbed to death. Police reported that she had been stabbed at least 25 times in her chest, neck, and back. Her "butchered" corpse was found under a thin layer of dirt and leaves. In February 2010 San Francisco police confirmed that DNA collected from that murder was sent to the Department of Justice and was subsequently matched to Carpenter.

He remains a suspect in the murders of Edna Kane and Barbara Schwartz.

Aftermath

Some have speculated that Carpenter wasn't technically a serial killer but a serial rapist who killed his victims to eliminate witnesses so as not to return to prison.

Carpenter's case provided the background for Joyce Maynard's 2013 novel, *After Her*.

A series of geocaching caches have been placed throughout Mount Tamalpais in commemoration of Carpenter's victims.

THE HILLSIDE STRANGLERS

NAOMI ROBERTS

Cousins Kenneth Bianchi and Angelo Buono, Jr. are collectively known by their media epithet "The Hillside Strangler". These two men were responsible for the murders of at least nine females, ages 12 to 28, during the late 1970s in Los Angeles, California, and Bianchi killed two more in Washington. After their first three victims did not gain much attention because they were prostitutes, Bianchi and Buono decided to abduct and murder middle-class "nice" girls. Five victims were found on hillsides in the Glendale-Highland Park area during Thanksgiving weekend in 1977 and the resulting panic led to the coining of the moniker "Hillside Strangler".

Lead Los Angeles Police Department homicide investigator Detective Sergeant Bob Grogan, along with his partner Dudley Varney as well as Los Angeles Sheriff's Department's Detective Frank Salerno, believed that the murders were the work of more than one killer but figured the less the murderers knew about what police knew the better.

Bianchi later moved to Washington where he murdered two more women before being caught.

Both Bianchi and Buono were convicted of multiple counts of first-degree murder and sentenced to life. Buono dies of a heart attack on 21 September 2002 while serving his time in Calipatria State Prison in Calipatria, California. Bianchi continues to serve his sentence at Washington State Penitentiary in Walla Walla.

Early Lives

Kenneth Bianchi

Kenneth Alessio Bianchi was born on 22 May 1951 in Rochester, New York, to a 17-year-old alcoholic prostitute who gave him up for adoption two weeks after he was born. He was adopted by Nicholas Bianchi and Frances Sciolono and despite a stable upbringing, Bianchi became a pathological liar at a very early age. Further, as a result of petit mal seizures he suffered at the age of five, Bianchi often daydreamt as if he were in a trance.

Bianchi suffered from insomnia and frequently wet the bed as a child (one of the triad symptoms of serial killers). Frances took him to the doctor on multiple occasions for his urination problem and being examined by the doctor caused Bianchi much embarrassment and humiliation. He also had a bad temper and was diagnosed with passive-aggressive personality disorder which is characterized by an individual who may appear to be enthusiastic about and actively comply with others' desires and needs while simultaneously resisting them, thus resulting in increased anger and hostility. At the core of this disorder is that the sufferer resents responsibility and instead of openly expressing his or her feelings, demonstrates said resentment through actions such as procrastination, forgetfulness, and inefficiency. Despite having a rather high IQ of 116, Bianchi was a chronic underachiever in school. When Frances took him to a psychologist, it was determined that Bianchi was overly dependent upon his mother.

On 2 January 1957, Bianchi fell off of a jungle gym and landed on his face. His mother then sent him to a private Catholic elementary school where he excelled in creative writing. In July 1963, Bianchi pulled down a six-year-old girl's pants after "spontaneously decid[ing] that he liked doing so".

His adoptive father died in 1964, thus leaving an unemotional Bianchi having to attend public high school where he joined a motorcycle club and dated frequently. His adoptive mother was forced to work and she was known for keeping Bianchi home from school for extended periods of time.

While in high school, Bianchi set high standards for his many girlfriends such as complete fidelity and outwardly absolute devotion; however, these standard did not apply to him.

He graduated in 1971 from Gates-Chili High School in Rochester and, soon after, married his high school sweetheart, Brenda Beck; however, the couple divorced after only eight months. Rumor has it that Brenda left without a word.

Bianchi enrolled at Monroe Community College to study police science and psychology after deciding that he wanted to become a police officer; however, after only one term he dropped out and then was rejected for several positions both in Rochester and, later, Los Angeles. Consequently, Bianchi worked a series of menial odd jobs, eventually becoming a jewelry store security guard for which he was fired for stealing and giving his girlfriends the stolen jewelry. He would steal from other employers over the years.

He then left Rochester and moved to Los Angeles in late 1975 at the age of 26.

Angelo Buono, Jr.

Angelo Anthony Buono, Jr. was born on 5 October 1934, also in Rochester, New York, to first-generation Italian-American immigrants originally from San Buono, Italy. His parents divorced when he was young and a five-year-old Buono moved to Glendale, California, with his mother Jenny and his sister Cecilia, where his mother supported the family by doing piecework in a shoe factory. Raised Catholic, this had no effect on Buono's development as a decent human being.

Buono displayed a very high interest in sex from a young age and when he was a teenager claimed that he had raped and sodomized number of girls. Buono idealized serial rapist Caryl Chessman, also known as "The Red Light Bandit", calling Chessman his hero but added that Chessman should have murdered his victims. He developed a deep loathing of women and desire to injure and humiliate them, including his mother who he would verbally abuse; however, he was emotionally tied to her until her death in 1978.

Buono began stealing cars and was sent to the Paso Robles School for Boys.

In 1955, Buono married his high-school sweetheart, Geraldine Vinal, who was 17 years old at the time, who he had impregnated; however, less than a week later he left her. She would later give birth to a son, Michael Lee Buono, on 10 January 1956. Buono filed for divorce and refused to pay child support or let his son call him "Dad". He was back in jail for car theft when his first son was born.

Later, he impregnated Mary Castillo who gave birth to his second son, Angelo Anthony Buono III, at the end of 1956 and then married her in 1957. The couple would have four more children: Peter in 1957, Danny in 1958, Louis in 1960, and Grace in 1962. In 1964, Buono was believed to have sexually assaulted his two-year-old daughter Grace; however, there is insufficient literature to know fully the circumstances of the allegation. Buono's second marriage to Castillo also ended in divorce that same year after she purported that he had been physically, emotionally, and sexually abusive toward her. In a last-ditch effort to reconcile with him, Castillo was "rewarded" with his handcuffing her and threatening to kill her at gunpoint. Castillo would later recount a night during the first year they were together where Buono tied her spread-eagled to the bedposts and "raped her so violently she was afraid that he was going to kill her" and "her pain seemed to him his greatest pleasure" and, thus, he had no qualms of hurting her and didn't seem to care that the children witnessed the abuse. He avoided paying child support again.

Buono married a third time in 1965 to a 25-year-old single mother named Nannette Campino and the couple had two children of their own: Tony in 1967 and Sam in 1969. Despite being treated as poorly as Mary Castillo had been, Campino feared for her life on a daily basis but stayed until he began to sexually abuse her 14-year-old daughter. Buono allegedly bragged that he raped his stepdaughter because "[s]he needs breaking in" and then turned her over to his sons for their pleasure. Campino finally took her children, filed for divorce, and fled the state in 1971.

Buono, again, was arrested for auto theft and was sentenced to one year in prison; however, due to his large family his sentence was suspended so he could work to support them.

Buono married yet again, on a whim, to a woman named Deborah Taylor; however, the couple did not live together, nor did they ever divorce.

In 1975, he became a car upholsterer and purchased his own place at 703 E. Colorado Street to live and work. Despite his abuse, cockiness, overbearing nature, and lack of good looks, Buono was considered very attractive by women, particularly younger ones who were usually naïve about sex so it was easy to convince them that his outrageous demands and proclivities were normal. Thus, he frequently forced women to engage in sex acts with him and began a relationship with a teenage girl whom he twice impregnated.

He was ugly inside and out; very coarse, vulgar, ignorant, selfish, and sadistic.

Bianchi and Buono Together

At the age of 41, Buono came into contact with his cousin Kenneth Bianchi, the latter who, in 1975, moved to California and in with his cousin. Bianchi found his older cousin with "dyed black hair, gold chains around his neck, a large gaudy turquoise ring on his finger, red silk underwear and a virtual harem of jailbait girls". Buono taught Bianchi how to use fake police badges in order to coerce free sex from prostitutes. When they needed money the two also became pimps for a short time until the two girls who worked for them—Sabra Hannan and Becky Spears—escaped after enduring relentless abuse by Buono. Bianchi, still desiring to become a police officer, applied for jobs at the Los Angeles Sheriff's and Glendale Police Departments but neither were hiring. He then procured employment with a title company and used his first paycheck on an apartment and a Cadillac, moving in with coworker Kelli Boyd. Boyd rejected his marriage proposal as she considered Bianchi to be very jealous, immature, and a liar; however, in May 1977 she told him she was expecting their first child together. The couple moved to an apartment at 1950 Tamarind Avenue in Hollywood.

Bianchi also rented some office space and set himself up as a psychologist with a fake degree and credentials. He did not have many clients and when Boyd found out she was outraged. During the "Hillside Strangler" investigation, Bianchi told Boyd he had lung cancer and was undergoing chemotherapy and radiation to explain for his work absences; however, this was a lie. One day, detectives came to his apartment to ask questions but were "favorably impressed" and did not consider him a suspect at that time.

The Murders

In October 1977, the two men committed their first murder together. Their M.O. was to cruise around Los Angeles and use fake badges to convince women that they were undercover police officers. After persuading them into Buono's car that the men said was an unmarked police car, the two would take their victims to Buono's house where they would rape, torture, and strangle them with their "signature" weapon—a garrote (a handheld ligature such as a chain, rope, or strap)—although some of their victims were reportedly killed by lethal injection, electric shock, and gas asphyxiation. Their bodies were thus disposed of outside, frequently in hilly areas.

Yolanda Washington, 19

19-year-old tall, leggy, African-American prostitute Yolanda Washington disappeared on 17 October 1977 from Cathedral City, California. She was found the next day dumped just outside Forest Lawn Cemetery, beaten, raped, and strangled with a piece of cloth. Her corpse was cleaned and there were faint marks around her wrists, ankles, and neck. Her body was posed in a grotesque sexual position.

Judith Lynn Miller, 15

On 31 October, 15-year-old Judith Lynn Miller, a runaway, was found in a La Crescenta-Montrose neighborhood, face up on a parkway in a residential area. The homeowner covered her with a tarp so that neighborhood children wouldn't see her. After the incident, that same homeowner relocated his family to another state.

The victim was small and thin, perhaps 90 pounds, with medium length reddish-brown hair. She had bruising around her neck. She had also been raped and sodomized and her body had been posed with her legs in a diamond-like position.

Los Angeles Sheriff's Department Sergeant Frank Salerno was called to the site. He noticed insect activity upon her skin and on her eyelid was "a small piece of light-colored fluff" that he saved for forensic experts. He surmised that she had been killed elsewhere and her body had been deliberately placed where it would quickly be found.

At her autopsy, the coroner determined that she had been killed around midnight and was raped and sodomized.

There was no missing person's report matching this latest victim so after a couple of days, Salerno had the newspapers run a small story on her with a request to contact the police if anyone could identify her. Still nothing. Salerno then took her picture to Hollywood Boulevard and showed it to hundreds of runaways, addicts, homeless people, and prostitutes. The name Judy Miller kept coming up as a young destitute prostitute. One man named Markust Camden—a self-proclaimed bounty hunter—told Salerno that he saw Judy Miller leave the local fish and chips restaurant at 9:00 p.m. the night before she was found dead. In fact, he would pick Buono out of a police photo lineup, but failed to recognize Bianchi.

Eventually, Salerno was able to track down the Miller family and got a positive identification. They had nothing useful to contribute to the investigation.

Elissa "Lissa" Teresa Kastin, 21

Lissa Kastin, 21, was working as a waitress at the Healthfaire Restaurant to pay for ballet lessons as she was an avid dancer. She also worked part time for her father's real estate and construction business. She was last seen leaving work the night of 5 November. She was found the next day near the Chevy Chase Country Club in Glendale on 6

November; which was also near to where Buono lived. She had been beaten, raped, and strangled to death.

Salerno compared notes with the Glendale Police Department and noticed similarities between his latest victim and this new one. Both bodies had the same five-point ligature marks—ankles, wrists, and neck—and had been dumped within six miles of each other. This latest victim had been raped but there was no evidence of sodomy.

When Salerno looked at the dump site he was confident that at least two men were involved due to the large guardrail between the street and where the body was found and the near impossibility that one man could have gotten her body over it alone.

Dolores Cepeda, 12 and Sonja Johnson, 14

After their early murders failed to attract much publicity, Bianchi and Buono decided to find some younger victims.

12-year-old Dolores Cepeda and 14-year-old Sonja Johnson were abducted in Highland Park, California, on 13 November. They had last been seen getting off a school bus heading home from St. Ignatius School and approaching a large two-tone sedan that, reportedly, had two men inside.

Both young girls were found on 20 November in the hills between Glendale and Eagle Rock, near Dodger Stadium by a young nine-year-old boy who was treasure hunting in the trash on the hillside.

Los Angeles Police Department Homicide Detective Dudley Varney had been called to this site.

Kristina Weckler, 20

That same day, 20-year-old Kristina Weckler was found on the other side of the same hillside where Cepeda and Johnson were found.

Weckler was a quiet, loving, and serious honors student at the Pasadena Art Center of Design and lived in Glendale.

She was found nude, raped, tortured, and strangled to death as evidenced by ligature marks on her neck, as well as around her wrists and ankles. She had blood oozing from her rectum and bruises on her breasts. Weckler was the first victim to show additional overt signs of torture; having been injected with Windex glass cleaner she had oozing injection marks on her arms.

Los Angeles Police Department Homicide Detective Sergeant Bob Grogan—Varney's partner—was called to this site. He noticed that there was no indication of any disturbance of the foliage in the area or evidence that the body had been dragged there. Grogan made a mental note that she likely had been killed elsewhere and then carried and dumped in this location by one or maybe two men.

At this point, police were entertaining the idea that there was more than one killer and that they were becoming increasingly more sadistic.

Jane Evelyn King, 28

28-year-old actress Jane King disappeared in Los Angeles around 10 November 1977, and was found near the Los Feliz off ramp of the Golden State Freeway on 23 November. She had been sodomized and strangled and her body was badly decomposed. After King was found, Los Angeles Police Department officials—in addition to Glendale Police Department and Los Angeles County Sheriff's Department officers—created a task force to catch the "Hillside Strangler".

Lauren Rae Wagner, 18

18-year-old student Lauren Wagner lived with her parents in the San Fernando Valley. Her parents had gone to bed on 28 November, expecting their daughter to return home before midnight. The next morning, they found her car parked across the street with the door ajar.

Wagner was found later that day in a wooded area near Glendale's Mount Washington area. She was lying partially in the street, nude, with ligature marks on her ankles, wrists, and neck. Wagner, too, had been tortured as the palms of her hands contained several burn marks.

At the dump site was also a "shiny track of some sticky liquid, which had attracted a convoy of ants". Police considered that if the substance was saliva or semen from the killer then, perhaps, his blood type could be determined, as tests on semen found inside the earlier victims revealed nothing. It was later found that Bianchi was not a secretor, in that his blood type could not be determined by other bodily fluids. DNA testing had not come into popularity at this time.

When Wagner's father questioned the neighbors, it turned out that the woman who lived in the house where his daughter's car was parked, Beulah Stofer, saw Wagner's abduction. Stofer said that Wagner had pulled over to the curb at around 9:00 p.m. and two men had parked their car beside hers. After some type of disagreement, Wagner "ended up in the car with the two men".

When Grogan went to talk to the neighbor, she told him that she had just had a phone call from a man with a New York accent who told her to "keep her mouth shut about what she had witnessed or he would kill her". Stofer also told Grogan that the car was a large dark sedan with a white top and that one of the men dragged Wagner from her car into his while Wagner protested, "You won't get away with this!" Stofer described one man as tall and young with acne scars while the other was older and shorter, Latin-looking, and with bushy hair. She said she was positive that she would identify them again. This statement rang true when she picked both Bianchi and Buono out of a photo lineup shown to her by Grogan.

Kimberly Diane Martin, 17

Tall, blonde prostitute Kimberly Martin, 17, disappeared from Echo Park, California, and was found strangled to death on 13 December 1977 on a steep hillside on Alvarado Street. Martin had worked for the Climax "modeling agency".

Police believed they had two reasonably good leads in this case. First, Martin's last "client" called her to 1950 Tamarind, apartment 114; however, this turned out to be a vacant apartment. Secondly, the murderer called from a payphone in the lobby of the Hollywood Public Library on Ivar Street. Unfortunately, nothing came from these leads.

Cindy Lee Hudspeth, 20

On 16 February 1978, 20-year-old Bible school teacher and secretary at an Echo Park church Cindy Hudspeth was found in the trunk of her bright orange 1977 Datsun B210 that had been pushed over a cliff on Angeles Crest in Los Angeles National Forest near La Canada. She had been raped and strangled, with the strangulation marks similar to those associated with the "Hillside Strangler".

Hudspeth was also a neighbor of Weckler even though the two women did not know each other. Interestingly, Bianchi also lived in the same apartment complex; however, this lead was never pursued even though both Grogan and Salerno believed that there was a good chance that at least one of the murderers lived in the Glendale area.

After this case, the lack of additional victims resulted in the disbanding of the "Hillside Strangler" Task Force.

Jill Barcomb, 18 (originally believed to be a Hillside Strangler victim)

18-year-old prostitute Jill Barcomb was abducted in Beverly Hills and found near the famous Hollywood sign on 9 November. Whereas it was originally believed that she was a victim of the "Hillside Strangler" because she had been raped, beaten, and strangled, in 2005, her death was conclusively proven through DNA analysis to have been committed by Rodney Alcala, the "Dating Game Killer".

Also, sometime in 1977, the two men gave Catharine Lorre a ride with the intent of killing her; however, when they learned that she was the daughter of famous actor Peter Lorre who played a child murderer in Fritz Lang's 1931 masterpiece film M, they let her go. She had no idea who the men were until they were arrested.

The two stopped killing after their ninth victim, Hudspeth (although at this time it was presumed they had ten victims with Barcomb), likely due to the birth of Bianchi's son and, as some surmise, that he had made some acquaintances within the Los Angeles Police Department who would take him on ride-alongs around the city, ironically, looking for the killers, and Bianchi could talk about nothing else while in police presence. On the night they had tried to abduct another victim, the two men got into a heated argument when Bianchi told his cousin that he had been questioned in the "Hillside Strangler" case. After Bianchi's confession about being questioned by police, Buono, furious, threatened to kill his cousin.

Bianchi's Washington Murders

Bianchi's girlfriend, Kelli Boyd gave birth to their son, Sean, in February 1978, and in March Boyd decided to return to her parents in Bellingham, Washington, as she was tired of both Los Angeles and Bianchi's lifestyle. After three months of pleading to be reunited, Boyd relented and Bianchi moved to Washington in May. Bianchi's role as boyfriend and father was relatively successful and he even took a job as a security guard, ultimately earning the trust of his supervisors. However, this way of life did little to alleviate Bianchi's murderous urges. Within six months he was actively looking for new victims.

On 11 January 1978, Bianchi lured two Western Washington University students—roommates Karen Mandic, 22, and Diane Wilder, 27—to a house he allegedly "guarded" under the pretense of housesitting. Once there, he raped, tortured, and murdered them.

On 12 January, police were informed that two female students were missing after Mandic's boss became worried that she didn't arrive at work that day. He did remember that she had told him she had accepted a housesitting job in a wealthy Bayside neighborhood from a security guard friend of hers. When former-priest-turned-Bellingham-Police-Chief Terry Mangan went to the girls' home he found a hungry cat, as well as the address of the home where they were to housesit. The name of one security guard kept coming up, as well as a record that Bianchi had used a company truck that same night, supposedly to take into the shop for repairs. This never happened. Mangan began to consider the fact that the women had met with foul play.

Police then went to the Bayside house and found a wet footprint. They also interviewed a neighbor who told them that a security guard asked her to check on the house except for the night the women disappeared because "there was special work being done to the alarm system and he didn't want her to be taken as an intruder".

After a press conference, a woman called police to report that a car had been abandoned near her home in a heavily-wooded area. In the car were the bodies of Mandic and Wilder. Both had bruising and had been strangled to death.

Mangan had the security guard picked up. He gave them no trouble. His name was Kenneth Bianchi.

There was ample forensic evidence in this case; most notably foreign pubic hairs on the girls and fibers from the house's carpet matching fibers on the dead girls' clothing and shoes. Additionally, when police searched Bianchi's home they found several items stolen from job sites where he worked.

Remembering back to the "Hillside Strangler" cases in Los Angeles—and knowing Bianchi had lived there—Mangan called the police departments in California who had worked on the task force. He spoke to Detective Frank Salerno to whom everything finally made sense. Detectives tirelessly worked to link Bianchi to the strangler cases and were confident that he was one of the murderers.

Investigation and Arrest

Bianchi was not as careful this time, having left significant clues, most notably his car with California license plates was seen and subsequently connected to the addresses of two Hillside Strangler victims. Without mastermind Buono, Bianchi didn't have the wherewithal to cover his tracks.

Bianchi was arrested the following day, on 12 January 1979.

Buono was arrested on 22 October 1979, after Bianchi told police about his cousin's complicity in the murders.

Trial and Conviction

Prior to his 1981 trial, Bianchi decided to plead not guilty by reason of insanity and claimed to have a separate personality named

"Steve Walker" who had committed the murders. After several interviews by experts specializing in multiple personality disorder and hypnosis, it was determined that he was faking. Immediately after Dr. Martin Orne mentioned to Bianchi that in genuine cases of multiple personality disorder there are typically at least three personalities, Bianchi created another alter ego named "Billy", shortly followed by two more. It was later determined that the name "Steven Walker" came from a student whose identity Bianchi had previously tried to steal to enable him to fraudulently practice psychology. Further, in Bianchi's apartment investigators found several psychology books which laid credence to Bianchi's ability to fake the disorder. He was eventually diagnosed with antisocial personality disorder with sexual sadism.

During trial, there was significant physical trace evidence against the two men; including fibers from Buono's upholstery from his home and workshop on two of the victims; an imprint of a fake police badge on his wallet; and hairs from rabbits he had raised on another victim.

Bianchi agreed to plead guilty and testify against his cousin in order to get leniency, albeit uncooperatively (evidence of his passive-aggressive personality disorder).

Judge Ronald M. George—who would later become California Supreme Court Chief Justice—said during Buono's sentencing hearing, "I would not have the slightest reluctance to impose the death penalty in this case were it within my power to do so. Ironically, although these two defendants utilized almost every form of legalized execution against their victims, the defendants have escaped any form of capital punishment." On an interesting side note, George's roommate at the time was author Darcy O'Brien who, four years after the trial, wrote a book about the case.

Both men were sentenced to life in prison.

While incarcerated, Buono married mother-of-three Christine Kizuka in 1986 while she was visiting her husband—and father of her children—who was in the cell next door to Buono at the Los Angeles

County Jail, serving 18 months for assault with a deadly weapon. She worked as a supervisor at the California State Employment Development Department.

Whereas the 64-year-old Bianchi continues to serve his life sentence at the Washington State Penitentiary in Walla Walla, Buono died of a heart attack on 21 September 2002 while serving life at Calipatria State Prison in Calipatria, California. Denied for parole on 18 August 2010, Bianchi will next be eligible for parole in 2025.

Aftermath

Bianchi is also a suspect in the "Alphabet Murders"—also known as the "Double Initial Murders"—which occurred in the early 1970s in his hometown of Rochester wherein three young girls were raped, strangled to death, and dumped in the wilderness. At the time he worked as an ice cream vendor situated near two of the murder sites. On 16 November 1971, ten-year-old Carmen Colon disappeared and was found two days later in Churchville, New York, 12 miles from where she was last seen. 11-year-old Wanda Walkowicz disappeared on 2 April 1973 and was found the next day in Webster, New York, off State Route 104, seven miles from Rochester. Finally, on 26 November 1973, Michelle Maenza, 11, disappeared and was found two days later in Macedon, New York, a mere 15 miles from Rochester. They were called the "Alphabet Murders" because not only did the young victims have the same initial for their first and last name but they were also found in cities which began with the same letter.

Whereas Bianchi has repeatedly tried to get his name cleared from these murders he remains a suspect because his vehicle was seen near two of the murder sites.

Another series of murders with similar circumstances occurred in California in the late 1970s and investigators have hypothesized that they are connected to the Rochester "Alphabet Murders". In 1977, Roxene Roggasch, Paula Parsons, and Carmen Colon (like one of the original "Alphabet Murder" victims) were found raped and dead.

Whereas Bianchi was tried for six murders, DNA exonerated him of the California "Alphabet Murders".

A 2008 movie entitled The Alphabet Killer was very loosely based upon the murders, and in 2010 a book written by Cheri Farnsworth called Alphabet Killer: The True Story of the Double Initial Murders was released.

In 1980, Bianchi started a relationship with a Veronica Lynn Compton, who was a defense witness during his trial. Compton, a cocaine addict who was fascinated by serial killers, was working as a scriptwriter in Hollywood. On one of her numerous visits with Bianchi while he was incarcerated, she gave him a copy of her screenplay entitled The Mutilated Cutter, about a female serial killer, and asked for this input. Compton grew increasingly fixated and allegedly fell in love with Bianchi. Later, she was convicted and incarcerated for attempting to strangle a cocktail waitress who she had lured to a hotel in a ploy to have the world—and authorities—believe that the real "Hillside Strangler" was still on the loose and that the wrong man was incarcerated. To make it look like an authentic "Hillside Strangler" murder, Bianchi manipulated and used Compton as a means to get out of prison by giving her semen of his smuggled out of the facility in a rubber glove to plant on the body. Despite that DNA forensics had not been utilized at that time, semen could still be analyzed to demonstrate the killer's blood type; however, Bianchi was not a secretor. The intended victim managed to get away and Compton was tried and convicted of first-degree attempted murder and sentenced to life. Compton was paroled from prison in 2003.

In 1992, Bianchi sued Catherine Yronwode for $8.5 million for putting an image of his face on a trading card. He claimed his face was his trademark. The case was dismissed with the judge saying that if Bianchi's face was, indeed, his trademark during the murders then he would not have tried to hide it from police.

In 2007, Buono's grandson, Christopher Buono, shot his grandmother—Mary Castillo who was married to Buono at one time—and then committed suicide. Christopher was unaware of his grandfather's true identity until 2005.

Bianchi and Buono are immortalized in film. The 1989 film The Case of the Hillside Stranglers—based on O'Brien's book—starred Dennis Farina as Buono and Billy Zane as Bianchi. In the 2004 film The Hillside Strangler, Buono was portrayed by actor Nicholas Turturro and Bianchi was portrayed by C. Thomas Howell.

The 2006 movie Rampage: The Hillside Strangler Murders starred Tomas Arana as Buono and Clifton Collins, Jr. as Bianchi.

In 2001 the Discovery Channel aired an episode of The New Detectives that revisited the murders.

Bianchi and Buono have also been mentioned several times on the television show Criminal Minds as an example of killer teams with psychopathic predatory sexual sadist personalities who murdered their victims together.

ROADSIDE STRANGLER

JASMINE GREY

When one envisions a serial killer, they think of a cold, calculating, heartless monster. As humans, some of us have developed ways to recognize other humans that are looking to cause us harm. If we look at a mug shot of famous another serial killer, like Charles Manson or Jeffery Dahmer, one could say that these men "look" like serial killers. Maybe it's because of their wild eyes, the way that they hold themselves, or the "creepy" feeling one receives from their presence. These factors are enough to make a person stay as far away from the killer as possible, but sadly, not all predators come with a warning sign. Michael Bruce Ross, later to be known as the Roadside Strangler, was a ruthless predator that slipped under the radars of the multiple women that he attacked, raped, and murdered. Detective Malchik, Ross' arresting officer, described this serial killer as, "There was nothing threatening about him, there was no signal to any of these people that there was a dark side or something that they should be afraid of. He was able to conceal that until it became time for him to attack these innocent, young women." Ross seemed to be an average-looking man of completely average-strength and abilities, but underneath his calm and normal exterior beat the heart of a man who struggled with his sadistic, sexual compulsions. When someone spoke to Michael Ross, they would say that he put off a very friendly and articulate demeanor seemed very well educated and kind, but it was merely a costume that he had created over a lifetime. The creepy part about Michael Ross, despite how honest and upfront he is about his murders, is the mystery behind his words. Is he being genuine or is this merely an act? Is he being honest or are we being deceived? His state of mind drifts from monotone claims to not possess any remorse for his monstrosities to genuine pleas for a chemical castration to reduce his perverse sexual desires. Michael Bruce Ross' case was a strange one, to say the least, and his mental condition will forever be remembered as a very dark part in Connecticut history.

The Childhood

Michael Bruce Ross was born on July 26, 1959. Among three other children, Michael Bruce Ross was born into the life of a middle-class chicken farmer. His mother Pat was impregnated in high school and forced into a shotgun marriage with Michael's father, Dan Ross. Needless to say, they did not go on to lead a very happy marriage. Pat Ross was a very mentally unstable woman, who underwent two abortions and was institutionalized twice. She abandoned her children and family once to run off with another man, but she soon returned to a depressing and emotionally unhealthy life on the farm. Pat Ross seemed to resent Michael more than the other children. His sister claimed that Michael received the brunt of their mother's aggression. Michael Ross claimed that he didn't remember his dark childhood or his emotional abuse-ridden family; he only had fond memories of working on his father's farm. The joyous memories of working on the farm centered on his peculiar job; Michael's job was to ring the necks of sick and malnourished chickens.

He recalled that he began to experience sexual fantasies around this time, like most boys his age, but they weren't anything like the hellish compulsions he faced in his adulthood. He explained his boyish daydreams as non-violent, although they might've been considered peculiar by most. In an interview, Michael describes his early, innocent fantasies of women, "I would kidnap women and take them to my safe place, and then they would fall in love with me, and never want to leave." It has been said that Michael was molested as a child by his mentally ill uncle while babysitting. As an adult, Michael Ross claimed that he did not remember this incident or his uncle at all; Michael was only six years old when the suspected uncle committed suicide. Whether Michael was too young to recall the incident or if he merely repressed the memory, the irreparable damage that comes along with molestation could be a very influential part of Michael's slip into sexual sadism. Despite his strange desires, his dysfunctional family, and his history of abuse, Michael was considered to be a pretty average child. As a teenager, he excelled in school, graduating as number sixteen in his high school class, and he eventually moved to Cornell University to study Agriculture and Life Sciences.

College Years

He continued to excel academically throughout his years at university. He studied Economics, Agriculture, and Life Sciences, and excelled in all of his academic endeavors. He joined the FFA (Future Farmers of America) and the Alpha Zeta fraternity. Ross' sophomore year roommate and Alpha Zeta brother, described Ross in 1977, "He kind of followed his own drum and went his own way." Michael never made any real connections in his fraternity, nor did he really make connections to anyone besides the long string of girls that he dated. In his college year, Michael Ross was rarely without a girlfriend, and he was rarely thinking about anything but. "There was always a certain obsession on his part regarding women," said his Alpha Zeta roommate, "That seemed to be such a big issue, a constant topic—needing a woman, needing to have a girlfriend. He would be obsessed about the relationship."

Ross claims that he did not experience truly violent sexual fantasies until his years at Cornell University. He especially did not begin to fantasize about raping women until his sophomore year in college. Michael Ross said that somewhere in his undergraduate years, he began to embrace the desires that brewed within him. He started his downward spiral with a very small step. He began to stalk his fellow students on campus. He would follow close by, making it known that he was behind her. "I would get a thrill by them knowing that I was following them. That they would be scared and that gave me a thrill," Michael explained his early experimentation with his predatory nature. When simply stalking the women wasn't enough, Michael eventually turned to towards rape. He hid in the bushes of Beebe Lake and raped a visiting student. Later, he attempted to rape another girl outside of the school observatory but failed. These assaults were only stepping stones to the full-fledged horror that Michael Ross was destined to cause. During his senior year at Cornell University, Michael Ross met Dzung Ngoc Tu, a Vietnamese student, and his very first murder victim.

The case of Dzung Ngoc Tu perplexed officials everywhere. She was found on May 17, 1981, in the Fall Creek Gorge. She died from a skull fracture and her body laid there for five days until she was discovered. It appeared to be a suicide, as if she had jumped from the bridge overhead and hit her head upon the fall, but there was no suicide note left at the scene. Close friends and family of Dzung Ngoc Tu claimed that there absolutely no signs of suicidal tendencies when she was alive and investigators found absolutely no reason for killing herself. Her body showed no signs of sexual abuse, there were no suspects, and the police had no idea that the culprit was actually Michael Ross, a man who was only connected to her by their similar majors. The case went cold when the police couldn't find a suspect. It wasn't until Michael Ross was already in prison for the murders and rapes of four other women when he confessed to murdering and raping a Vietnamese girl that went to his school in New York.

The Attacks and Murders of The Roadside Strangler

Michael Ross chose his victims merely off of chance and circumstance. If he encountered a woman that was in a vulnerable position, he felt this undeniable compulsion to attack. "There's nothing they could've said or done. It was me, it wasn't them," Michael Ross admitted with a solemn tone of voice, years after his final attack, "They were dead as soon as I saw them, I think."

Michael claimed that he only attacked women to relieve pressure that built up from his personal relationships with the women in his life. When he was working in North Carolina, shortly after he graduated from college, Michael recalled that he had a very difficult visit from his fiancé, which caused him to attack a random woman shortly after he dropped his fiancé off at the airport. He noticed a woman walking on the sidewalk with a baby stroller, so Michael pulled the car over and attacked her, using her own child as a weapon. "I told her that if she didn't do what I wanted, I would smash the baby's head against the wall of the house," Michael described in an interview, he seemed as if he were on the verge of tears, "I've always said that I never understood why these women never really resisted me. I'm not a big, strong guy, but nobody ever seemed to fight. I've always just contributed it as I must say something like that, or similar to it, to the other victims." He raped and strangled the woman, then left her for dead in her driveway.

On June 15, 1982, a 23-year-old woman named Debra Smith Taylor was attacked by Michael Ross in a park. He pulled her over where no one could see them, raped her, and forced her to roll over on her stomach; he then strangled her from behind. The young girl's body was discovered much later in a dried up river bed, only a few miles away from the location of another of Ross' victims, Tammy L. Williams. "Each time I killed, I made myself believe that I wasn't going to kill again," Michael Ross explained in an interview. It wasn't very long before he killed again.

His next attack occurred on a cold Thanksgiving Day in 1983. Michael Ross encountered Robin Stavinsky outside of Norwich State Hospital. He saw the woman in a vulnerable position and he took advantage of the situation. He forced the 19-year-old girl into a wooded area and demanded her to remove her clothing. Ross forced himself on the young girl then told her to roll over on her stomach. He strangled her from behind until the innocent Robin Stavinksky died in his hands. "Serial killers like to strangle their victims and that is, I guess, the most common form of killing because there's more of a connection there. It's more real and it's not as quick," Michael Ross explained why he enjoyed strangling so much. After he was finished with her, he covered her body with leaves and left her for dead.

The Roadside Strangler struck again on Easter Sunday, 1984. April Brunias and Leslie Shelly were hitchhiking on the side of the road when Michael Ross happened to drive their way. He pulled over and offered the young girls a ride. The girls did not find Ross threatening so they got into his car and asked him to drop them off at the next gas station. When Michael passed the gas station, one of the girls drew a kitchen knife and threatened to stab him. In an interview Michael Ross explained what happened next, "I almost drove off of the road, I was so surprised. I don't know what I said, but I said something and she gave the knife to me. It obviously scared her." He parked the car at Beach Pond and used a cloth to bound both of the girls by their hands and feet. He put Leslie Shelly in the trunk of his car, then dragged the girl named April a few feet away from the car. He raped the young girl, flipped her over onto her stomach, and strangled her until she died. He then took Leslie out of the trunk and did the same thing to her. "The smallest one, Leslie Shelly, has always bothered me more than the others. I think it was because she was so small, I think it was because she was so cooperative, and I think it was because the way she was killed was so close to the fantasy. That was the one that was... it was like it was fantasy," Michael explained. The girls were only fourteen years old when they were murdered.

It was a summer afternoon, around three o'clock on June 13, 1984, when the Roadside Strangler committed the murder that would finally get him caught. He was driving home from work when he passed Wendy Baribeault, who was walking down the side of busy Route 12 in Libson, only a few miles away from his home. Michael Ross pulled the car over and began to speak to this 17-year-old girl; he repeatedly invited her to his company picnic. After a little bit of conversation, Michael forced the beautiful, young girl over a stone wall and into the woods. "When I attacked her, I don't believe that I was in control. I don't think I would've been able to stop," Michael Ross explained his mental state during this attack, "I didn't really feel anything. I knew what was going on and I saw what was going on, but it was more like watching an old film..." Michael then raped the innocent girl and strangled her, just like the others, then entombed her in the stone wall that lined the busy road. The road was so busy, in fact, that there were several eyewitnesses to the attack.

The Investigation of the Roadside Strangler

The police had absolutely no leads on the murderer (a.k.a. The Roadside Strangler) that had taken Connecticut by storm. That was until Wendy Baribeault's body was found. There were dozens of eye witnesses to her attack and composite drawings were created that matched the facial features of local Michael Bruce Ross. Witnesses also noted that the attacker was driving a blue Toyota. Michael Malchik, the investigator assigned to the case, compiled a list of several thousand blue Toyotas. This tiny bit of evidence eventually led investigators directly to Ross' house, which was only three miles away from the location of the crime scene. Michael allegedly dropped hints that he was the murderer upon speaking to the police. "It all had to end," Michael Ross explained. It wasn't long before Michael was called into an interview with police in 1984. After a few hours of grueling interrogation, Michael Bruce Ross confessed to all crimes that he'd committed in Connecticut, but left out the murders in New York. "It's a mystery to me to this day, but it's typical of him," stated Detective Malchik, "Here he is, confessing to six murders, and he thought enough ahead not to tell us about the New York ones. Looking back at it, it's obvious he was thinking of something. He was always thinking two steps ahead. He's got his own agenda, but I couldn't for the life of me tell you what it is."

When Michael confessed to the murders, he seemed very sorrowful and remorseful, but he claimed not to feel a blink of remorse, "I don't want to say that I don't have any remorse, it's just like they weren't real..." Michael explains his feelings towards hid victims in a later interview, "I can't see them as I was killing them, so when I say I don't have any remorse, that doesn't mean that I don't have any regrets, or wish that didn't happen, or there was something that I could do to bring them back or anything – I don't have any feelings towards them. I feel like I should be tormented by them - by what they look like when I was killing them – or tormented by what was happening immediately before I killed them – but none of that's there. None of that's there at all."

"The only time he said he was sorry, was that he was sorry for getting caught," Michael's arresting officer explained, "He (Michael Ross) told me matter-of-factly, he said, 'If you hadn't caught me, I would've just kept on killing, again.'" This eerie statement by itself was enough to put the Roadside Strangler to death immediately, but his strange nature kept investigators questioning his motives behind being so upfront and honest about his heinous crimes. Did he secretly want to get caught? Was this all part of some big plot to instill his insanity?

Anne Cournoyer, Michael's correction counselor, described his mannerisms as he spoke of the horrible crimes that he committed, "One minute he's very, you know, looks like he on the verge of crying, and the next minute he's sort of giggling nervously - or sadistically – you just really don't know. You think that maybe, it's out of nervousness, but he could be getting pleasure out of talking about it."

A full-scale investigation of Michael Bruce Ross' life led to the realization of his wavering mental stability. Michael Ross explained that he could never recall the faces of his victims, even directly after the murders, "You'd think that if you killed someone, you would have the face imprinted in your mind and that you wouldn't be able to get it out of your mind – I don't have that. I never had that," He explained, "The only faces I could see was what was in the newspapers a few days later when they were missing. You know, the high school pictures and 'anybody know where this girl is?' type of thing. When I think of them, that's the picture that I see. I don't see them as they were when I killed them. If you had stopped me right after and gave me a composite drawing of like twelve pictures - you know - some blondes, brunettes, whatever – I wouldn't have been able to pick them out. Even immediately after I killed them."

The names of all eight women were: Dzung Ngoc Tu (25), Paula Perrera (16), Tammy Williams (17), Debra Smith Taylor (23), Robin

Stavinksy (19), April Brunias (14), Leslie Shelley (14), and Wendy Baribeault (17). He was only charged with the murders of the four Connecticut women because the murders of Dzung Ngoc Tu and Paula Perrera took place in New York. He was sentenced to death on July 6, 1987, but remained on death row for eighteen years after his sanity was called into question.

The Curious Case of Michael Bruce Ross

Michael spent the next eighteen years of his life caught in a battle of the Connecticut justice system. In court, a team of psychiatrists flocked to the defense of Mr. Michael Ross. After a parade of psychiatric evaluation, Michael was deemed mentally unwell, due to his dark childhood and his undeniable compulsions. Dr. Fred Berlin, the well-known co-founder of the Johns Hopkins Sexual Disorder Clinic, testified that Ross was struggling with a mental disorder called sexual sadism. Meaning that he gained sexual excitement from the pain and suffering of others. This discovery alone was not enough to save Ross' life, but Michael's claim to lose all self-control during the murders was enough to set back his execution date. Connecticut's state psychiatrist reluctantly agreed that Ross was not mentally capable enough to be responsible for his own actions, and therefore, it was not right to put him to death. Dr. Robert Miller wrote in a private letter, "I can't see how I could testify against psychopathology playing a sufficient role in defendant's behavior." Although this letter was never presented in court, Michael Ross' death sentence was overturned in 1994 and a new sentencing hearing was scheduled in 2000.

Michael Bruce Ross spent most of his time on death row writing about the mental disorder that took hold of his entire life. Michael claimed to have no control over his actions due to his compulsions. He described his sexual sadism as "a mental illness that drove me to rape and kill" and "made me physically unable to control my actions." During his time in prison, Michael still fell victim to his compulsions. It was impossible for him to control his sexual desires, so he spent the first few months of his incarceration reliving the murders. He claimed that he would fantasize these murders over and over again, hurting himself and causing sores from compulsive masturbation. It wasn't very long before he begged for some type of relief from his sexual desires, which came in the form of chemical castration. Ross was given medication that was designed to lower his testosterone levels and it finally relieved him from his sadistic compulsions. Thanks to this medication, Michael Bruce Ross was finally able to think clearly and he was able to see the true nature of his crimes.

The team of prosecutors naturally disagreed with the defense's attempts to lessen his blame. Prosecutors claimed that if he were unable to control his desires, he would've made less calculated attacks. It was reasonable to assume that Ross experienced these sexual desires constantly, which means that he probably experienced these feelings while in public places, or places where his actions could've been seen and reprimanded. Instead, Ross chose his victims very carefully, only acting when the girls were vulnerable and alone. Disproving the defenses' claims more so was the fact that Ross' hid their bodies after the attack, which further strengthened his blame and the case that he knew precisely what he was doing when he was doing it. "I'm not saying I wasn't there or it was multi-personality or any of that type of crap," Michael Ross later explained the strange fog he experienced while he murdered these innocent women, "I was there and I did it, but I wasn't one hundred percent there." To set light upon Mr. Michael Ross' guilt, Prosecutors relied on the "Policeman at the Elbow" test: would Ross have committed the crime even if a policeman had been standing next to him?

The defense team immediately disagreed with the statement that all of Ross' attacks were calculated and well thought out, considering the murder of Ms. Wendy B. who was murdered next to a busy road with several eyewitnesses, "When I attacked her, I don't believe I was in control. I don't think I could've stopped." Michael spoke about the murder that eventually resulted in his incarnation. "Could he control himself? Well, two juries rejected that," Detective Malchik recalls, "As the state's attorney said at the trial if Ross was so out of control, why didn't he just rape the girl in between the yellow lines of Route 12? He made it simple for the juries to understand."

John Blume, a professor at the Law school and co-founder of the Cornell Death Penalty Project, noted the how the jury in Ross' case did not take the opinions of the psychological experts seriously. "The thing that's disturbing," Professor Blume stated, "is that even when the experts all say your client is insane, juries will still reject it." Despite the team of psychologists on Ross' side, claiming that he was completely unable to stop himself from committing these monstrosities, the jury chose not to believe them.

Somewhere in the eighteen years of Michael Ross' incarceration, he decided that he did not deserve to live anymore. Shortly after Michael wrote a story called "It's Time for Me to Die", he reconnected with a woman named Kathy Jaeger, who served as his pastoral advocate that converted Ross to Catholicism. Ross wrote in a newsletter that Jaeger, "was able to breach my defenses and was able to touch my soul as no one else ever has." He later called Ms. Kathy Jaeger "the most important woman in my life" and claimed that "If I were a free man, I would ask her to marry me." Although Kathy rejects his claims to romance, she continued to support Michael Ross throughout his decisions.

After she entered Michael's life, there was a great shift in the nature of his case. Michael was done fighting for his life and the mental condition that wreaked havoc on his entire existence. After his original death sentence was overturned in 1994, the court ordered a new penalty hearing, but instead of going through the hearing with his public defenders, Ross acted as his own attorney. He worked with prosecutor C. Robert Satti to created what was deemed as "death pact" that allowed the imposition of the death penalty without a penalty hearing. "Please allow me to go into the courtroom . . . to accept the death penalty as punishment for my actions," Ross wrote in a letter to Satti. "I'm not asking you to do this for me, but for the families involved, who do not deserve to suffer further and who, in some small way, might gain a sense of peace of mind by these actions and my execution." The "death pact" was rejected by the judge as a "short cut" involving a human life, so Michael Ross flip-flopped back into his old ways. Ross returned to his defense team and reverted back into fighting for his life, claiming that his crimes were merely a product of his mental illness. He was resentenced to death soon after.

Jaeger said that Ross's sudden acceptance of death was a sincere attempt to provide closure for the families of his victims, "He told me, 'You know I don't want to do this. But I have to.' He just really felt anguish over what he had done. Really, really harsh anguish and self-loathing. Contrary to media reports, he doesn't want to die. He wishes that the justice system got it right years ago and gave him life sentences because he does have a mental illness. And the sad thing is, if they had done that, the families of his victims wouldn't have been re-victimized [by the ongoing appeals]. Michael is trying, in essence, to save them from any more of that."

Whether his acceptance of the death sentence was sincere, or not, Michael Bruce Ross was sentenced to death by lethal injection on May 13, 2005. He chose not to speak any last words before his death and died peacefully in the execution chair. Some family members believed that his death was too peaceful. Debbie Dupuis, Robin Stavinsky's sister, stated that she thought she would "feel closure" but instead just "felt anger" as she watched Ross simply lay there, go to sleep and die.

The state of Connecticut finally decided to end the life of the Roadside Strangler and put an end to the anguish that the families had to endure. After a very tragic and dark lifetime, Michael Bruce Ross and his sadistic compulsions were finally laid to rest.

Conclusion

Michael Bruce Ross is the type of cold, calculating, manipulative killer that we only read about in horror novels. His crimes almost seem too heartless and brutal to be true, but the victims of the Roadside Strangler would tell you that he is nothing but a cruel reality. In only a few years, Michael assaulted a countless number of women and murdered eight. Although he was only charged with four murders, Ross was forced to withstand eighteen long years of debate over his life sentence. In prison, he transitioned from a vicious killer who was truly non-remorseful for his brutal crimes to a man who seemed to genuinely regret his life choices and the pain that he subjected. Towards the end of his life, Ross begged for removal from his troubled existence, not only for himself but to end the long and grueling process of the legal system. Despite his transition into humanity, Michael Bruce Ross never took full blame for his actions. He flip-flopped between blaming his childhood, his compulsions, and his interpersonal relationships for these terrible crimes. He claimed to never feel any guilt or remorse for his actions, simply because he wasn't completely there while they were taking place. During these attacks, Michael claims that he was under some type of spell, some type of fog that completely disconnected him from his actions. He was completely able to murder and rape these innocent women without feeling guilt or remorse, or even being able to recall the very faces of his victims', only moments after their attack. Michael Ross was an extremely troubled man who suffered from a very extreme case of sexual sadism. Michael explained his cruel, heartless, attacks with vivid details and an undetached tone of voice. The scariest part about his calm demeanor is the monotone way that he described the way he stole the lives of these young, innocent women. He speaks as if he were not responsible for killing these beautiful and young women, although he willingly confesses to the murders. He claimed that he was merely a victim of his sexual compulsions since his college years and the women he attacked were merely in the wrong place at the wrong time. Whether his desires were really uncontrollable or if it was merely an excuse, Michael Bruce Ross' case remains to be one of the most perplexing cases in American history. His mere mental condition was enough to perplex the entire state of Connecticut – how could this well-spoken, articulate man with such a great personality, commit these terrible crimes? Why didn't anyone notice his decline and stop it? What was it that made this seemingly normal man snap into the Roadside Strangler? Although the answers to these questions are uncertain, they definitely are unnerving. Michael Ross was created by circumstances, by his dark upbringing, and a lifetime of people letting him slip through the cracks. Everyone saw him as an average, everyday college student, so no one thought to ask. The woman that he murdered were sadly only stepping stones into the downward spiral into his sickness and they were eventually caused the end of his vicious, murderous cycle.

CLASSIFIED AD

RAPIST

65

VICTORIA MANN

Criminal psychologist and behavioral scientist often find themselves debating on the effects of nature versus nurture when dealing with people who cause harm to others. The argument stems from the possible theories of a person's physiology and biology affects or is affected by the environment in which they are raised. For serial killer and rapist Bobby Joe Long, both nature and nurture shaped who he became later in life. Long was born with medical issues that would plague him later in life. His medical situations would increase as he experienced one after another after another accidents and incidents leaving him with damage to his head and physical facial deformities. These physiological issues would then be compounded by a broken household with an unconventional parenting, a life riddled with early exposure to sexuality, drugs and alcohol, and abuse. As Long passed through the years, his reactions to the world around him and his treatment of people would escalate until he would spend almost two years raping, beating, and murdering a string of women before the law finally stepped in an put in behind bars.

Bobby Joe Long was born on October 14, 1953 in Kenova, West Virginia to Joe and Louella Long. Long was born with Klinefelter Syndrome, meaning he had 47 instead of 46 chromosomes, one extra X chromosome. This medical diagnosis would be an early, but overlooked, warning sign about Long's development both physically and mentally. With the extra X chromosome, males often see delayed puberty, growth of breast tissue, smaller testes, and hormonal imbalances. With a starting point already giving Long problems that would affect him psychologically and medically, the young boy had an unfortunate beginning. Klinefelter Syndrome also causes delayed and slower learning abilities, language development barriers, and usually a more introverted and emotional social reaction to people and the situations around them.

Joe and Louella Long divorced in 1955. Joe stayed in West Virginia while Louella Long took Bobby Joe and moved to Miami, Florida. This would be the beginning of a back and forth living pattern for Long, and where his issues with his mother would start to blossom. Later it was established that Long was often left with the landlord while his mom was out for long amounts of time. It is not clear whether she was always working, or if this is when her reputation for being out with different men had started. Though only two years old, Long would look back as this being when his mother began habits that would later color their relationship.

In the summer of 1957, Long had the first of many accidents that would cause further damage to him physically and result in mental repercussions. That summer Long was pulled under the waves at the beach by the strong undertow. Long nearly drowned and would make the comment later in interviews that his mother was "too busy looking at other men" to be paying attention to him and preventing the incident. A year later, in 1958, Long fell off of a swing while playing. He received the first of many concussions and ended up having a stick puncture his eyelid. His mother took him back to West Virginia and began seeing his father again. Though his mother and father would have an on and off again relationship, they always returned back to Florida in less than a few months or weeks. By fall of 1959, Long was beginning first grade in Miami, though he failed to pass and would repeat first grade the next year. During 1959, Long had another accident. While riding his bike he hit a parked car, throwing him over the vehicle. Several of his teeth were knocked out and Long ended up with another concussion. The following year would be spent going back and forth between Miami, FL and Kenova, West Virginia while his parents tried to re-establish a relationship. He completed first grade in West Virginia.

1961 was a rather rough year for Bobby Joe Long. During the spring he was hit by a car. His face was directly impacted by the front bumper knocking him unconscious and ending with him hospitalized in West Virginia. In the fall, Long ran out into traffic and was hit by an oncoming car. Once again he would have more teeth knocked out, but this time he would be left with a deformed jaw from the accident. At another point during the years of 1960-1961, Long was riding a pony when he fell off. Though he was not hospitalized, the resulting head injury left him dizzy and nauseous for quite some time afterwards. In 1962 Long once again found himself returning to the hospital. This time was from a fall from a fence that caused a laceration on the left side of his head, resulting in stitches. Bobby Joe Long already had the misfortune to be born with a brain altering health issue, having a drowning incident and having six head injuries in less than five years would cause a build-up of scar tissue in his brain that wouldn't be noticed until he had a psychiatric evaluation after his arrest. Ironic, as Long spent the majority of his jobs as an X-Ray technician in varying hospitals.

By 1963, Joe and Louella Long decided to end their marriage again. Louella Long took Bobby Joe and moved back to Florida. This time they would live in a house with several of her family members. So many family members lived in the home that Bobby Joe Long was forced to share a bed with his mother. His home situation in combination with his deformed jaw made fourth grade a difficult time for Long. He was repeatedly bullied and made fun of by his peers. Long's mother began working two jobs, one as a waitress and another as a bartender. When she wasn't working she was usually with a different man. Between her job and social life, she began dressing in revealing and provocative clothing. Long began taking out a lot of his aggression on his mother. He verbally began abusing her, often referring to her clothing and lifestyle as being "slutty." Long felt neglected, as well, due to his mother's absences and time spent with the other men.

Louella Long bought a new home in Hialeah, FL in 1965 for herself and her son to live in. The parade of different men seemed to not only continue, but escalate in Long's opinion. Long began skipping school and becoming more socially withdrawn and more verbally abusive towards his mother. In 1966 Long killed the family dog. His reasoning was that his mother care more for the dog than she cared for him. He once stated that "she fed the dog fillet mignon and I only got hamburger." Long now had a separate room from his mother and began detaching himself from her. He met Cynthia at this time, the girl that became his best friend and confidant. Long also began developing breast tissue, gynecomastia, a side effect of the Klineflter Syndrome, and had to have them surgically removed. Despite developmental setbacks, he had consensual sex for the first time in 1967 with Cynthia.

Bobby Joe Long committed his first crime in 1968. He and one of his friends stole a car. The charges were dropped, though, and Long was never punished for the act. In 1970 he was arrested for the first time for minor theft. Later that year he began working for Arc Electric on a part time basis. Long dropped out of tenth grade twice but would re-enroll the following year. At this point, Long's abuse towards his mother started to become physical. The next year, 1971, he was accused of rape. The charges were dropped and the victim was assumed to be lying would insufficient evidence was found to corroborate her story. Shortly after starting school again, Long was expelled. His view of women was already shaded by his mother and what he experienced in dealing with her lifestyle, and now his feeling towards authority were also colored darkly, causing more disturbing thoughts and feelings for Long to deal with when his mind was already suffering from multiple destabilizing factors.

Long enlisted in the army in 1972 with hopes of becoming an assistant electrician. After finishing basic training, he was stationed at Homestead Air Force Base in Homestead, FL. Despite having the army to help give Long a better direction in life, his inability to stay away from criminal activity persisted. In one day he received seven vehicle related tickets. Though he did have many small setbacks, Long was able to eventually get his GED with the army. Throughout his hardships, his relationship with Cynthia grew. They were married in January of 1974 in the chapel on base. Unfortunately, despite his luck seeming to improve, Long was in a severe motorcycle accident in February. Long ended up spending several months in the hospital suffering from another head injury, damage to his shoulder, and extensive damage to his leg. Doctor's contemplated amputation but concluded the leg would be able to heal enough that it would not be necessary. After enduring one head injury after another since he was a child, Long began to show more obvious signs of brain damage. His sexual libido began to increase, to an extent in which the nurses notating him masturbating over five times a day while still hospitalized. He also began demanding more sex of his wife, Cynthia.

Due to the damage to his body and the possible brain injuries, Bobby Joe Long was medically discharged from the army in August of 1974, after serving less than two years. Long and his wife moved off base into a trailer, where they would raise their newborn baby boy. Since he was recovering from the accident and now unemployed, Long had ample time on his hands. He began using newspaper ads to look for women to satisfy his new sexual appetite. Long did begin to attend Broward Community College in order to try to complete his electrician training he was hoping to accomplish while in the army. Long was once again trying to bring some semblance of balance back into his life, but now the build-up of what he had lost, his inability to handle emotions well, and the behavioral issues brought on by his brain damage, Long began taking out his aggression on his wife. He was arrested for domestic battery against Cynthia.

Despite their growing problems, in 1975 Bobby Joe and Cynthia welcomed a new baby girl into their family. They move to Ft. Lauderdale in an attempt to find work and spend the next several months moving around and looking for jobs, even in West Virginia. Towards the end of 1976, Long's parents help them buy a house in Hollywood, FL. Long returned to community college and was finally able to become a certified electrician in 1977 and even receive his associate's degree as an x-ray technician in 1978. In November of the following year he got a job at Parkway Medical in Miami as an x-ray tech. His success was once again short lived as 1980 rolled around. In June, Cynthia filed for a divorce. She listed the marital issues as abuse and financial instability. Long moved into an apartment in Ft. Lauderdale alone. Shortly after, his bad luck continued as he lost his x-ray technician job. Long then moved in with a friend, Susan Replogle, in order to have someone to split rent with. The stay was short before he moved again, this time with a friend named Ted Gensel. Susan Replogle, then, moved in with the two men.

1981 brought with it, even more problems for Bobby Joe Long. Susan Replogle reported Long for rape. The charges never held, though, due to insufficient evidence, again. Two weeks afterwards, Replogle was beaten and thrown down the stairs by Long. Around this same time, Long began picking up and raping prostitutes. In October, Susan Replogle filed an assault and battery charge against Long. One month later, Long was charged for sending obscene material to a 12 year old girl in Tampa, FL. Phone records and mailing envelopes left Long with no choice but to plead no contest.

Long spent the majority of 1982 traveling and looking for work. During the first half of the year he went to California to get a commercial driving license through a commercial driving school. He then returned and tried to find work as a truck driver. Eventually he ended up back in West Virginia, living with his parents. Both of his parents stated that he spent most of his time there sitting around and not actually looking for work. It wasn't until February of 1983 that he finally got employment as another x-ray tech at Huntington Veterans Administrative Hospital in West Virginia. Though his fellow employees were quoted saying he was "polite" and "a good worker," Long was fired in April for making his female patience undress when it was not medically necessary for them to do so. In June, Long bought a 1979 2-door maroon Dodge Magnum and moved back down to Florida.

In the Tampa area, Long was once again hired as an x-ray tech. This time he worked at Humana Hospital on a temporary basis. In August he met Elise at the hospital. Long began dating Elise, and due to her devout religious nature, even began attending church with her. Long seemed to be trying to put his life back together again and even sent $4000 in back child-support to his ex-wife Cynthia. Long's past, though, caught up with him. In September, Long was giben a guilty verdict on the assault and battery charge against Susan Replogle. Bobby Joe Long was furious at the conviction and wrote several letters to the judge and the charge was changed to neutral pending further evidence. In November, Long was given his sentence to his no contest plea in the exposure of obscenities to the 12 year old girl. He spent two days in jail and was put on probation. In the early part of 1984, Long was officially acquitted of assault against Susan Replogle. Long was still able to continue a relationship with Elise throughout this time.

On March 6th, 1984, Bobby Joe Long committed his first pre-meditated rape through his habit of browsing newspaper ads. Long responded to an ad for a house that was being sold. He arrived at the Port Richie home with materials to tie up the woman who was showing the house. When the tour of the home reached the bedroom, Long pulled a gun and tied her up, raped her, and then stole her jewelry. This would become Long's source of income as he repeated the tactic numerous times and even quite his hospital job to continue his criminal career. His girlfriend, Elise, never questioned where he got the money or the jewelry from.

It was on March 27th, 1984, that Long's new habit would go to the next level and become his first murder. Long picked up Artis Wick in Tampa as she trolled the streets. She was found strangled a while later. Long claimed she had not satisfied him and he got angry and strangled her. In April, Long abducted Mary Hicks and forced her at gunpoint to drive him in her Jaguar. Mary crashed the car, escaped, and went to the police. Long was later charged for damages and only received probation. Though he was getting by on his thefts, Long got a job in May at Gulf Bay Electric in Tampa as an electrician. A new crime spree was formed, though, and Long was no longer satisfied by just raping and stealing from his victims.

May 4th, 1984 was when 20 year old Ngeun Thi Long (no relation to Bobby Joe Long) was offered a ride home by Bobby Joe Long. Ngeun had recently quit her job as a stripper and was walking the streets at the unfortunate time when Long was prowling for his next victim. Long took her to a wooded area. His MO was established during this murder as he made her strip naked, lie face down on the seat, he tied her hands behind her back, and then raped her. Long then took her out of the car and beat her repeatedly before strangling her with left over rope. Her body was found nine days later, face down, naked, hands still tied behind her back, and her legs spread wide. The rope was still around her neck.

Bobby Joe Long was once again fired on May 23rd. Women he worked with and those that came into contact with him stated that he was rude and overtly perverted in his nature. Other employees stated he was obsessed with porn and his work station was plastered with pornographic material. Long would begin a steady of pattern of committing rapes and thefts on women he found in the classified ads on a near daily basis and raping and murdering women he came across on the streets as often as several times a month.

Michelle Simens' body was found on May 27th, 1984. The 22 year old was a cocaine addict and prostitute that Long picked up on Kennedy Boulevard and taken to the local "lover's lane." Long proceeded with Michelle as he did with Ngeun, making her strip down, lie face down on the seat, tied her hands and raped her from behind. Michelle Simens fought back, though, as Long tried to strangle her with a rope. In his frustration and anger, Long pulled a knife and stabbed her numerous times and finished by slitting her throat several more. Her body was found with the rope still around her neck. Her clothing was tossed into the nearby trees. Investigators would get several pieces of evidence from her murder scene, though. Among these were red fibers, human hair, bare footprints, tire tracks, and semen.

June 8, 1984 was when Long found his next victim, 22 year old Elizabeth Loudenback. Her body was found in an orange grove in Brandon, FL. Long had maintained his MO with the abduction and rape of Elizabeth. This time he sodomized her as well. He then forced her to redress and get back in the vehicle. According to Long, she wouldn't stop crying and saying that she was hurting and so he strangled her. She had her debit card and a piece of paper containing her PIN in her wallet. Long used these to make multiple withdraws from her account throughout the night. Her body was discovered on June 24th, badly decomposed and weighing less than 25 pounds. She was fully clothed and still had the rope Long strangled her with around her neck.

Bobby Joe Long spent June 14th with his children in an overnight stay. By the end of the month he was able to get a job at Tampa General Hospital as a x-ray technician. In July he was finally sentenced for his abduction of Mary Hicks. Long was charged $1,500 in damages and three years of probation. Long moved into a new apartment, but once again his luck would not last. In September he was fired from Tampa General Hospital for failing to get the advanced certification he needed to maintain his job as an x-ray technician. He had already built up a bad reputation with female colleagues and patients for his perverted nature. He did meet another woman, Ruth Allende, who he began dating and had a normal sex life with. Unbeknownst to her, Long was a rapist and murder with few signs of changing his habits any time soon.

Chanel Devon Williams was an 18 year old Long picked up on September 30th, 1984. Long proceeded as he had done before in forcing her to undress, placed her face down on the front seat, and raped her. He beat her and attempted to strangle her but Chanel was extremely athletic. Long once again lost his temper, this time he pulled a gun and shot Chanel Williams in the back of the head. Long tossed her body under a fence and threw her clothing out of his window as he drove away, causing it to get caught along the fence and the sign for the ranch he had taken her to. Her body was found on October 7th while Long was raping and killing Kimberly Hopps, another 22 year old. Five days later, Long repeated the pattern with Karen Beth Drinsfield. Her body was found in an orange grove a day later on October 14th. Another woman, Vicky Elliot, also went missing during this time period. Two weeks before Kimberely Hopps body was found, Long was once again spending the night with his ex-wife and children. Shortly after his visit, Long would take another woman, but this time would be very different.

On November 3rd, 1984, Bobby Joe Long kidnapped 17 year old Lisa McVey. Long forced McVey into his car at gunpoint and made her perform oral sex on him as he drove her back to his apartment, something he had not previously done. Once at his home, Long raped McVey, but seemed to quickly regret what he did. According to McVey, Long showered her and referred to her as his girlfriend. He started telling her how pretty she was and trying to say nice things while being delicate with her. Long did try to sodomize McVey, but stopped when she said it hurt too much. Long brushed her hair and clothed her and even made her a sandwich and had her eat. Long's gun was on the nightstand, but he unloaded it stating that he did not want to do anything stupid or to be tempted to use it. Long then blind folded McVey and took her back to his car. He gave her a description of a random black man and told her to say that guy was the one that had taken her. Due to the blindfold being loose, McVey was able to see the car and the landmarks around them while they drove. Long reached a parking lot and helped McVey out of the car, kissed her goodbye and left. McVey ran home and made it there by 4:30am. She woke her father and told him what all had happened. Her father immediately went to the police.

On November 6th, 1984, the skeletal remains of Virginia Johnson were found. The police at first believed that she had been dismembered, but further analysis showed the skeleton had been torn apart by scavenger animals. Four days later, on November 10th, 21 year old Kimberley Swann was driving erratically; she had a history of driving under the influence of drugs and alcohol. Bobby Joe Long coaxed her to pull her car over to the side of the road. Long offered Kimberley a ride and she got into his car. The two ended up arguing, and Long became furious with the woman. He strangled her and pushed her body out of the car onto the side of the road. Her body was found two days later. The body of Vicky Elliot was found on November 16th.

Police got a break on November 15th, 1984. Bobby Joe Long was pulled over when his vehicle matched the one police were looking for. Due to lack of immediate evidence, police took a photograph of Long and his vehicle and released him under surveillance. The next day, the same day

Vicky's body was found, police got a warrant for Long's arrest listing his crimes as abduction, kidnapping, and involuntary sexual battery in the case opened for Lisa McVey. Bobby Joe Long began confessing almost immediately. On November 18th, 1984, Long was charged with eight counts of murder and sexual battery, nine counts of kidnapping, and violating his parole. Three days later Artis Wicks body was found. On November 28th the judge ruled the case needed to be seen in front of the grand jury. On December 5th, 1984, Long was charged with the murder of Virginia Johnson.

Bobby Joe Long was held in prison while the courts sorted through the plethora of murders and rapes to build a case against him. On June 18, 1985, a private investigator gave police a suicide letter, confessing his crimes, that Long had written. Bobby Joe Long was moved into the infirmary for close observation and to protect him from self-harm. A psychiatric evaluation was given to Long in February. The doctor's conclusions were consistent with the brain injuries Long had received over the years, along with mental illnesses that he inherited from his parents and that resulted from the Klinefelter Syndrome. Bobby Joe Long was a sexual sadist with bipolar and manic depressive psychosis. The scar tissue and constant damage to his brain over the years had caused organic personality syndrome and temporal lobe epilepsy that caused him to go into altered states of consciousness. The doctor explained that these lapses were usually what occurred when Long would go into bouts of anger and begin beating, or in some cases stabbing and even killing, women.

The Klinefelter Syndrome already left Long with hormonal issues that caused him to have over reactions and overemotional feelings in different situations. The bipolar disorder was believed to have been inherited from his mother. Long then had the repetitive accidents and occurrences of damage to his head causing constant tears and swelling that then would scar over, building up the tissue and resulting in more problems. With Long's mother having the on and off again relationships with his father, the questionable taste in men, clothing, and work and their relationship souring as it did, Long built a very negative view of women. His anger then became more sexually oriented and resulted in his sprees of rape and murder. Long often felt disgusted by women and degraded them when he could, making them little more than a sexual item to him.

As the year carried on, and despite the psychological evaluation and results, Bobby Joe Long was charged in the various crimes he had committed, from the abductions to the rape and thefts to the rape and murders. Each sentence being more stern than the last. When Long had confessed, he had asked for a lawyer and one had not been given to him. Though he did confess that same day, this would cause issue in the first trial. The first major trial was for eight of the murders and Lisa McVey's kidnapping, abduction, and rape. On September 24, 1985, Long agreed to a plea bargain and plead guilty to all. He received 26 life sentences total and would not have any possibility of parole. He also received seven life sentences that, after the first 25 years, he could attempt to appeal for parole. Though his confession was thrown out, the evidence in the case clearly matched Long's vehicle to the red fibers and witness reports and the semen and prints to Long himself. In 1986, the Michelle Simms trial began in Tampa, Florida. The evidence allowed the district attorney to ask for the death penalty and it was granted. Several more cases began to arise and were sub sequentially tried and Long was convicted. Long did appeal the first degree murder and death penalty verdict for Virginia Johnson. The case went forward to an acquittal and became stagnant.

Currently, Bobby Joe Long is on Florida's death row. Despite several attempts at appeals, acquittals of some of the random rape cases because of lack of evidence, the majority of Long's sentencing equates to over several thousand years behind bars and is capped with the death penalty. The fiber analysis came under fire in the nineties when it was discovered that one of the lab technicians was not following protocol. Although Long and his defense team tried to utilize this to his advantage, the plethora of other incriminating evidence along with witness testimony and his confessions made little difference in the effect of the fiber analysis in the case results. It was unfortunate that Bobby Joe Long seemed to be cursed at birth. Being born with an extra x chromosome, his Klinefelter Syndrome caused him psychological issues from his hormonal and emotional imbalances very early in life. Suffering from multiple head injuries and then deforming facial injuries, Long had a very difficult time socially interacting with people. He found himself being pulled back and forth between Florida and West Virginia with his parents' constantly changing marital situation. He then had the difficulty of living with a parent that was gone a lot, saw different men constantly, and living in difficult households, including one in which he would share a bed with his mother as he began the early years of puberty. Long did have chances at redemption. He met Cynthia, the first person he ever confided in, his first love, his first wife, and the mother of his children. He seemed to keep contact with her, long after their divorce, and even tried to stay current with child support and visiting his children. Even though he went on to have several other normal relationships and even good jobs, Long would sabotage each one and always fall back to his habit of using newspaper classifieds to take advantage of women. When rape and theft wasn't enough, Long then began his abduction, rape and murder of women he found on the streets. Bobby Joe Long had a very difficult life and it is hard to say whether he would have led a different life if not for the Klinefelter Syndrome and multiple injuries as a child. Could he have had a normal childhood and became a normal functioning adult? Or was the damage and hormonal issues just an added fuel to the raging fire that burned within him? Psychologists still debate the issues of nature versus nurture and how much that weighs in on criminals like Bobby Joe Long. The only definitive information is that he will never again have the chance to try to be a different person, but he will also never again have the chance to terrorize or end another woman's life.

THE SCUMBAG

Alexis Malone

Gary Charles Evans was born to Roy Evans and Flora Mae Lee in Troy, New York on October 7th, 1954. He had an older half sister named Robbie who was the product of a previous relationship for his mother. There was also a family friend named Jo Realm who was considered his "older sister."

Gary wore thick glasses in school and was teased. His father also subjected him to regular beatings whenever Gary disobeyed him. He would beat the boy unmercifully with a leather strap, making welts form across his back.

Roy was an Army corps pilot until being discharged. He was aimless after his military service ended, working as a bartender but then becoming permanently disabled after flying head first through a car windshield in an accident. He would then take out his life's frustrations on his family, particularly Gary.

Roy Evans would often make his son stay at the dinner table until he finished his food. There were occasions when he would tie him to the dining room chair and force feed liver to Gary.

Gary would also allege that his father would sexually assault him, "doing vile things" which he "wouldn't wish on anyone."

His parents would have violent arguments and forced Gary to stay in his room, confining him like the future prisoner he would become. He would not be allowed to watch television, draw or do any other pursuits which may have interested him.

His "big sister", Jo Realm, would give him food, passing dinner plates from her room to his because their apartments were so close.

His mother, Flora, worked primarily in retail and in a factory. The factory she worked for closed down, however, so Flora turned to housekeeping to make ends meet.

Flora suffered from mental illness and attempted suicide several times. She would often make these suicide threats in front of both Gary and his sister, traumatizing them. On one occasion, she waved a gun around, threatening to kill herself. When her husband tried to intervene she accidentally shot him in the shoulder.

Flora would have scars on her wrists from slitting them so many times. She would bring men home and make Gary stand watch outside the door while they had sex.

His mother would continue her suicidal ways, one time she threatened to jump off the roof of their apartment building but Robbie tearfully talked her out of it. Sometimes Flora would wander to the railroad tracks and stand in the crossroad, waiting for the train to come run her over.

Robbie would again talk her out of it, convincing her how much she and Gary loved her.

"The whole nature versus nurture argument comes to bear in looking at Gary's background," forensic psychologist Wendy Lipscomb said. "He was abused by his father physically and perhaps sexually. This coupled with the mental abuse by his mother made the wiring in his brain abnormal, without question. He had no one to turn to for guidance really other than his sisters Robbie and big sister Jo. He would remain wired that way for the rest of his life, having more of an ability to relate to women more so than men. His victims would all be men."

Gary's life of crime would start at the age of eight. He had stolen a ring worth over $1,000 in addition to comic books and toys. His mother was a thief herself, shoplifting items at will.

The constant bickering between his parents would end when Gary was fourteen years old as they would finally divorce.

Flora would remarry and divorce four more times over the next three years. She had Gary would move to Potterville, New York but her new husband would prove to be an abusive alcoholic. Later, she would marry a man named "Jim" who was another alcoholic. Going through another divorce, Flora declared herself to be a lesbian and got a girlfriend.

Gary would be forced to live with his older sister (Robbie) and her husband.

His brother-in-law was prone to violence, abusing both Gary and his sister. This would force Gary out onto the streets where he would fend for himself, ping-ponging between the streets and his mother's home.

Gary began to support himself by whatever means he could, mostly by stealing from drug dealers to obtain money. At the age of sixteen, he broke into a home and serve three months for the burglary.

By the mid-1970s, Gary would spend a lot of time being homeless. He would break into cars, trucks, and abandoned buildings. Eventually, he would live with two childhood friends. One was a man named Michael Falco who reportedly tortured and sexually abused animals. The other was fellow thief, Timothy Rysedorph. Gary would live in a shed behind their apartment before he moved in.

"They played baseball or stick ball or something when they were little kids," Dana Rysedorph, the wife of Tim said. "They rode their bikes together and did the things that little kids do. And they may have shared an apartment when (Rysedorph) was about 19."

"But since I started dating Tim, I never saw the man (Gary Evans)," Dana said. "The first time I saw the man was when the police showed me a mug shot. I'd like to know when Tim had time to fit this in. All he ever did was work and spend time with us. But because he knew (Evans, he's supposed to be side-by-side with him?"

Having these two partners in crime, Gary would step up his thievery, becoming adept at appraising antiques and jewelry. He would run a con on local antique dealers, pretending to be an expert. He would study their storefronts for openings in which he could later break in.

Both Falco and Rysedorph would assist him in these antique store burglaries. The trio would bypass store alarms by tunneling outside the walls in order to enter the store undetected.

Evans would be convicted for fifteen antique-store robberies over the course of his life.

"Gary was the ringleader of the group of friends from around his block," Lipscomb said. "He held no emotions for them, however. He viewed them as a means to an end, people that he could use and later discard if they proved to be a liability. For the most part, he was a loner. He could sleep out in the woods and go for long periods of time without the need for any contact. He didn't so much have friendships with men as much as he had partners in crime."

Gary would have many girlfriends, mainly Deirdre Fuller. The two would date from 1977 until 1990 but the relationship would be a tumultuous one. He was okay with her dating other men, as long as they were Caucasian. When Deirdre began dating a black man, Gary became enraged.

He wanted everything he had ever given her back.

"I would like to kill a woman and a nigger," he would later state to friends.

On January 13th, 1977, Gary would be caught burglarizing a home in Lake Place, New York. He would be sentenced to four years in prison, being held at the Clinton Correctional Facility in Dannemora, New York.

Six months later, his father would die of throat cancer while Gary was held in jail.

He would serve two years of the four year sentence until his release. When he got out, he went back into the same pattern of petty theft with Tim Rysedorph and Michael Falco.

They would use their apartment as a fencing headquarters for all of their stolen goods before renting out a storage unit.

The trio would evade capture for almost a year until Gary was stopped by police and caught with a few hundred dollars in stolen goods.

Gary, still on parole, was immediately sent back to prison, this time to the old Rensselaer County Jail in downtown Troy, New York.

On this occasion, however, he would befriend some Hells Angels inside who engineered an escape. Gary would be captured five hours after fleeing the prison and be punished with solitary confinement.

Gary would remain in prison and be denied parole this time around.

The New York State Department of Corrections then transferred him to Attica State Prison which housed the most violent criminals. Gary was spared being placed in the general population but it is here that Jim Horton, the chief investigator of his crimes, believed that Gary turned violent.

He would work as an informant for Jim Horton, telling them of impending petty crimes that he knew were about to take place, setting up a large drug bust with a man named Archie Bennett.

"Gary was a good talker when he wanted to be," Lipscomb said. "He knew he could charm and he couldn't. By running cons in the antique business, he quickly learned the art of negotiation. He was able to parlay this skill in getting a 'job' of sorts as an informant."

Gary would be released from prison on December 29th, 1982 but once again return to his old pals, particularly Michael Falco.

Two months later, however, Gary's mother would die in a freak accident. She fell on some ice while entering her car and hit her head on the bumper.

Gary grieved but soon returned to his life of crime with Falco and Rysedorph. He would break into a home on Easter, 1983 and once again be arrested.

Back in prison, he remained there for a year before being set free on a "conditional release program." This mandated that he had to be on his best behavior for the remaining nine months of his sentence.

Gary would scoff at the court order. He went back to burglarizing homes as soon as he was released. Teaming up with Falco, the two thieves would not get caught over the next nine months.

On February 16th, 1985, the duo would go to East Greenbush, New York in Falco's brown Plymouth. They had two large duffel bags, a police scanner, a rope ladder and other burglary tools.

Parking behind an antique shop, they propped up a portable toilet and made their way to the top of the roof.

Gary and Falco then dropped down from a hatch on the roof. In just minutes, they would fill the duffel bags with whatever they could; gold, jewelry, valuables all tallying up to $15,000.

They climbed back out of the store and whooped and hollered at the size of their stolen booty.

A cop, however, pulled up behind them as they were about to leave.

He asked what they were doing behind the building and the two men casually explained that they had to "take a piss."

The cop took their identification down and let the two thieves go, Gary's charm enabling them to get away.

"At this point of his life, Gary was a career criminal," Lipscomb said. "He was intelligent, with the ability to meticulously plan a robbery. He could walk into a store and see the ways in and out, ways in which the ordinary person would never dream. But for all this intelligence he could not see the trajectory that his life was on. He was only intelligent in certain things. He did not have a clue when it came to living a sustainable life. He was one a road destined to prison and true to like minded criminals he did nothing to get off that path. He embraced it instead."

On April 21st, 1985, Gary went to Troy, New York to sell dope to two marijuana dealers. The dealers gave him the money ($12,000) and when they went to his trunk to retrieve the marijuana, Gary sprinted away. The two men gave chase and Gary circled back around, getting into their vehicle and speeding away.

The dope dealers then called the police, telling them that Gary had robbed them of both the money and the car by gunpoint.

Making his way into Cohoes, New York, Gary would run a red light.

A cop immediately pulled him over but Gary thought the officer was stopping him for the robbery. Gary then threw his gun and fake identification out of the vehicle before sprinting out of the car. The cops eventually found him and sent him to the Albany County Jail.

On July 1985, he was sentenced to another two to four years before being moved to the Renssaler County Jail.

Upon his release, Gary would commit his first murder in shooting his burglary partner, Michael Falco. Rysedorph had told Gary that Falco had stolen some jewelry from him. Rysedorph said that Falco had given the jewelry to a female friend. This enraged Gary and he decided to kill his childhood friend.

Gary would use a .22 caliber pistol with a homemade silencer (he would make the silencer himself with parts of a screen door and duct tape)

He enlisted the aid of Rysedorph to put Falco's body in the trunk of his own car, wrapping the corpse up in a sleeping bag.

The two then drove to Lake Worth, Florida to visit Gary's sister Robbie.

They would bury the body near her house and would stay in Florida. It would later be revealed that Rysedorph had lied and the truth was that he had stolen the jewelry.

"Gary had now made the progression from small-time thief to drug dealer and murderer," Lipscomb said. "This does fit the psychological profile given his background. He endured parental abuse and would torture animals (he once tied up the tail of a cat and set it on fire.)

Bouncing in and out of jail had no doubt lowered his inhibitions. Whatever remorse or hesitation he felt was now out the window. He would commit whatever crime he felt would be necessary and his mindset would be the same. 'Don't get caught, don't get caught.' If anyone around him was careless or looked like they would prospectively betray him, they would be killed. Falco was the first of many."

Gary would then return to prison after being caught for another burglary. His sister Robbie would write Gary in prison. She wouldn't visit and hardly ever wrote so Gary was scratching his head upon receiving her letter. Robbie would write that someone was calling her, disguising their voice as Gary's. This person would say that he was into bestiality and bragged about having sex with farm animals.

It was yet another episode in an increasing series of bizarre occurrences in Gary's life. While in prison, he began fantasizing about an ex-girlfriend, Stacy, someone he had not seen in over fifteen years. Gary wanted to find her and then kill anyone who got in his way who tried to stop him. Gary would never admit to being homosexual but it was reported that he had relationships with transsexuals in prison. Later, he would have a friend come over and discover his collection of homosexual magazines, dildos and other gay sex toys.

In December of 1986, Gary would be moved to the Clinton Correctional Facility. He was placed under protective custody as he convinced authorities that the Hells Angels were out to kill him.

Gary would complain that he was being held until March of 1988 when his release date should have been in December of 1987. He then wrote a letter to Torri Ellis (Falco's common-law wife) and inquired if she heard anything about Falco, knowing full well that he killed the man.

While in prison, Gary would befriend David "The Son Of Sam" Berkowitz who was a serial killer of young girls. David would call Gary "The Great Tricep King" in reference to his muscular arms. The serial killer would anger Gary, however, when he gave him a muscle magazine which featured a black bodybuilder. David would later apologize to Gary as he didn't realize how racist his fellow mate was.

The two would lift weights together but during one session Gary would call his new friend "David Berserk-o-witz" which would end up in a shouting match between the two.

His troubles in jail didn't end with the Son of Sam. Beefed up with the weight training, Gary entered a child molester's cell and "body slammed him all over."

He was then sent to solitary confinement for two weeks before being once again released in March of 1988.

"During this last foray in prison, Gary would come out even more sociopathic than before," Lipscomb said. "He now had a new physique, building up his arms and back. He would use this to intimidate drug dealers in the area and his future partners in crime. It was a classic case of 'show me your friends and I'll show you your future.' He had spent the majority of his adult life amongst criminals in jail. Now, armed with a new physique, he would be ready to take his game to another level."

Gary would befriend a new partner in crime, Damien Cuomo, and the duo would pride themselves on being intelligent thieves. The pair would be smarter and more prolific than before, even going so far as wearing shoes that were three and four sizes too big to throw off the investigators.

As part of his parole, however, Gary had to get a job. He always thought jobs were for suckers and that they were "too hard."

Investigator Horton seemed to take pity on him, however, and set the lifetime thief up for different jobs. Gary would work at a cemetery digging holes but couldn't make it past the first five days. Ironically, while he was in prison, he was forced to work. Gary was an amateur artist and the prison authorities made him make greeting cards. This earned him $7 a week which he used to buy junk food with Twinkies being his favorite.

After the cemetery job fell through, Gary got a job at a garden nursery where he would do all of the heavy lifting. He worked sporadically, more comfortable with commiting burglaries on the side.

Gary would stay out of trouble for almost a year until March of 1989. He and Cuomo were on their way to a job when a cop pulled them over. The officer searched their trunk and found ski masks, stun guns, a police scanner, walkie-talkies, crowbars, screwdrivers, duct tape, ropes, handcuffs, gloves, hats, maps, and a book on police radio frequencies.

The cop did not discover that the duo had hidden stolen goods in the door panels and under a carpet in the trunk.

He did have enough to book the lifelong criminals, however.

"Gary was a hopeless case at this point," Lipscomb said. "He was advancing in age and could never adjust to a normal nine-to-five. He had disdain for an honest days work and preferred the quick hit of a burglary. At this point, he is also a travesty of the criminal justice system. He had been in and out of jail over twenty-three times, they still can't pin the Falco murder on him, yet they keep letting him out of jail."

After a brief jail term, Gary would be released and immediately pick up where he left off with Cuomo.

On September 8th of 1989, they would kill Douglas Berry, a store owner asleep in his shop after hours.

Gary and Cuomo did not realize that Berry was still in the store when they had broken in. Berry was asleep but the breaking glass awoke him. He discovered the two men in his store but Gary would shoot him once in the head with his .22 caliber gun.

The shot would be fatal.

The duo ran out of the store, leaving Berry's body in full view.

Gary would monitor the news with anxiety until police arrested another man for the murder. This innocent man was soon released, however, and the police remained in the dark in who shot Douglas Berry.

Three months later, Gary would kill his partner, Damien Cuomo. He believed that he should have gotten more money for their robbery as he only got $15,000. He shot him three times in the back of the head after handcuffing Cuomo's hands behind his back. He wrapped up Cuomo's body with a shower curtain, blanket and tied it all together with a rope.

Gary had dug a hole at his place weeks before and hid Cuomo's body inside, covering it with a makeshift door and dirt.

He then went on the run to Florida with his girlfriend, bringing her along so it looked as if he was not hiding something.

In the summer of 1990, he still had Stacy (his teenage girlfriend/fantasy) on his mind. It had been over fifteen years since he had seen her and he daydreamed about taking her away from her husband

Gary followed up on his warped fantasy. He showed up at her workplace but Stacy made it clear that she did not want anything to do with him. He then went back to New York and in October of 1981, he would kill another jewelry shop owner named Gregory Jouben.

This killing would be pre-planned.

Gary entered the store and pretended that he was looking to by some jewelry. He waited until Jouben looked down to retrieve a piece when Gary shot him three times in the back of the head with his .22 caliber pistol.

Gary had placed a pillow case around his gun to catch the shells. He would then steal over $60,000 worth of valuables from Jouben.

In a panic, the now confirmed serial killer would flee to Colorado but then return. He placed the gun that he killed Jouben with into a metal box and buried it in the back of Albany Rural Cemetery.

Always the opportunist, Gary would steal a marble bench from the cemetery (it weighed one thousand pounds) and bring it back to New York, successfully selling it days later. He would also steal a 300-pound brass eagle which stood atop an obelisk marking Col. Ernest Ellsworth's grave.

"With the killing of Cuomo," Lipscomb said. "Gary no longer had a regular partner. So he had to strong arm some of his burglaries as was the case with the Jouben murder. He wouldn't be able to break in by himself so instead he takes a more direct approach. This new bold attitude bespeaks of his growing arrogance. Even if he goes to jail he will come right back out. He's a man that will steal anything that isn't nailed down. Even if it is nailed down, he'll try and take out the nails."

In March of 1993, Gary would break into the bathroom window of the antique shop of Kathy Alexander. He would steal diamonds, gold, a rare handbag valuing up to $20,000.

For whatever reason, Gary had a fetish for hanging out in cemeteries. He would try to steal another marble bench from a cemetery but this time graveyard security spotted him. Once again, he would be throw in jail but only for a month.

Seeking new opportunities, he would break into the Norman Williams Public Library in Woodstock, Vermont and steal the Birds of America book by James Audubon. This was bad news for Gary as not only was the book priceless but a federal judge was on the Board of Trustees for the library. He would give himself up for stealing the book and be sentenced to 27 months in jail. Gary would serve only thirteen months and upon his release, he would kill his former partner Timothy Rysedorph.

Rysedorph was helping Gary clean out their storage facility where they kept their stolen goods. Gary then turned the gun on Rysedorph, killing him.

Rysedorph would reported missing by his wife, Dana.

He had called her earlier from a Dunkin Donuts restaurant and said he would be home within the hour. His car would be found the next day.

Rysedorph would leave a note on the table for his family which said "Have a good day. See you later. I love you."

Dana and his then nine year old son Timmy would hope for the best to no avail.

Gary had cut up Rysedorph's body with a chainsaw, sectioning the limbs off in five pieces. He bagged each body part then placed them into cardboard boxes. He then drove to a hill in Brunswick, New York where he buried the boxes in a shallow grave. He tossed the gun and chain saw into the Hudson river.

Gary would cover his tracks, deciding to call Lisa (Cuomo's girlfriend) and inquire about Tim Rysedorph.

"Lisa? Lisa Morris?"

"Yeah?"

"This is Lou," he said in an angry voice. "Where's Tim (Rysedorph)?"

"Who's this?"

"This Lou."

"I don't know. Who are you?"

"I'm a friend of his from work. I'm returning his call."

"I haven't heard from him."

"Hmmm," Gary said. "He might be in some trouble, girl. He might be in some trouble."

Still on probation, Gary disappeared for seven months. He would call Lisa again, telling her that what happened to Mike (Falco) probably happened to Tim (Rysedorph) but that Cuomo was probably living it up in the Carolinas. He would befriend the woman, giving her all kinds of stories of why Cuomo was not coming back. He needed a place to stay and she allowed him to live there.

Police would finally trace the killing of Rysedorph back to him. He would be captured in Jonesbury, Vermont.

Gary would confess to the five killings and then be transferred to Albany County jail where he would remain in protective lock down.

He would then lead detectives to where he buried the bodies of Tim Rysedorph and Damien Cuomo.

Investigator Jim Horton then made Gary call Lisa Morris again and tell her that he had killed Cuomo after having her believe for so long that he was still alive.

The woman was flabbergasted. She could not believe that Gary had lied to her and for so long.

Gary was transferred to the Rensselaer County Jail in downtown Troy but nixed the idea when they realized that that part of the jail was under reconstruction. He was considered a serious flight risk and admitted to both investigator Horton and Jo Rehm that he will try to escape.

The district attorney decided to try him as a capital offender and have him executed by lethal injection.

Gary would have his hearing at the Albany Jail in Colonie, New York. During his transport, he kicked out the window of the police van while the vehicle was traveling across the Troy-Menands bridge over the Hudson river.

"They were traveling about 60 miles an hour when he apparently threw both his feet through the window and shattered it," Troy Fire Chief Robert Essigan said. "Somehow he jumped out the window, over the guardrail and into the water."

Evans had his hands shackled behind him and his feet chained together as he was riding in the rear of the caged U.S. Marshals van.

The trip was only supposed to last twenty minutes. A second vehicle with two additional deputy U.S. Marshalls followed as Evans made his way back to the Rensselaer County Jail.

He then dove onto the roadway through the side window. The vehicles screeched to a halt.

Deputies then chased Evans who had "hobbled" over to the side of the road before jumping off the bridge.

Witnesses would call the police as they initially thought Evans was a construction worker with his orange coveralls.

Gary had taken off his handcuffs and flipped off the US Marshalls as he fell to his death.

"There was really nothing they could do," Essigan said. "This guy was quite an escape artist. He was good, and I guess this was his spectacular ending."

He left behind a suicide letter expressing regret that he would not be able to spend time with Doris Sheehan, the woman he loved.

His final words were sent to lawyer Randolph Treece, whom he addressed in a letter. "No lessons here are learned, onto a better place now," Evans wrote. "My friends are happy and I'm already there with Canis Minor (a star of the constellation Orion) and a Beautiful Blue Moon with a smile, stars surround me and peace and love are mine. They can't be taken or touched."

"I win," were the last words he wrote, underlining "win."

His body would be recovered and during the autopsy the medical examiner would find a razor blade and a paper clip taped to his ankle under his sock.

Gary also had a handcuff key stuffed up his left nasal passage with another razor blade shoved very deep inside his nose.

Relatives of his victims felt no remorse when they learned of Gary's suicide.

"It couldn't have happened to a nicer guy," Mary Deeb said, the sister of Michael Falco. "I'll probably go to hell for that but I can't help it. That's the way I felt. It's terrible to feel so relieved that someone jumped to his death but I cant help it."

"I'm going to tell you, when I saw him on TV and he had this very smug, arrogant, non-remorseful look on his face. I knew he's no good," Sal Falco said, the older brother of Michael. "I think there's a higher power that says it's time for you to stand in my court and there's a tougher jury up there."

"Forgive? Forgive him for killing my brother? No way. There's no reason to kill my brother. He didn't do anything wrong. He didn't deserve that kind of a sentence."

"He killed Michael when he was 26," Elaine DiMauro said, Falco's former girlfriend and mother of his two children. "He had a family and two children to look forward to. I was hoping he would go to jail. Justice still hasn't been served."

"I think the gates of hell are opening wide open for this man. The fires are burning pretty crisp. I hope to God they suffocate him."

SMELLY BOB

OSCAR VALDEZ

Robert Black (Smelly Bob)

Robert Black, also known as "Smelly Bob" was a Scottish pedophile and serial killer who preyed on young girls in the United Kingdom. Between 1981 and 1986, Black was convicted of the kidnap, sexual assault, and murder of four girls—plus the kidnapping and rape of another young girl and the attempted kidnapping of yet another—between the ages of five and 11 and was sentenced to life in prison with a minimum of 35 years. Black is also suspected of being responsible for the murders of 12 other girls between 1969 and 1987 in England, Ireland, and continental Europe. Black died of natural causes on 12 January 2016 while incarcerated at HMP Maghaberry, just weeks before he was to be charged with the murder of another of his victims.

Early Life

Robert Black was born on 21 April 1947 in Grangemouth, Stirlingshire, Scotland, the illegitimate son of Jessie Hunter Black who was 24 at the time and an unknown father whose name was never put on Black's birth certificate. Jessie earned a pittance as a factory worker and was in no position to care for a child, let alone an illegitimate one which carried with it a large social stigma. So, when he was six months old Black's mother had him fostered. He was subsequently raised by experienced, middle-aged couple Jack and Isabel Tulip who lived in Kinlochleven. Black initially adopted their surname and lived with them until 1958 when his foster mother died; his foster father having already passed away when Black was five. When Margaret died, Black was only 11 years of age.

In the meantime Black's mother married Francis Hall, had four more children who never even knew that they had a half-brother, and moved to Australia. She died in 1982 without ever having any contact with the son she gave away.

Locals remember how young Black was usually heavily-bruised as a child; however, Black himself does not remember how he sustained most of the injuries. He did recall how Margaret used to lock him in the house as punishment for poor behavior or would spank his bare bottom with a belt. During the night, Black feared that there was a monster under his bed and he suffered from a recurring nightmare that featured a "big hairy monster" in a cellar full of water. When he awakened, he found that he had typically wet the bed, for which he was invariably beaten.

In school he was referred to as "Smelly Robbie Tulip" and is remembered to this day as "aggressive and slightly wayward" as well as being a loner with a tendency to bully. Black preferred the company of younger children who he could easily dominate. Instead of joining a "gang" of classmates his age, he started his own and all of the members were several years younger than he. Compounding the problem was that Black demonstrated "sudden, mindless violence perpetrated against those physically less able than himself."

The local bobbie, Sandy Williams, remembers Black as a "wild wee laddie" who "didn't give a damn" or have respect for authority and that he had a "dangerous spirit" and "needed a smack round the ear to keep him in line." However, the entire time Black lived with the Tulips he was never in serious trouble; just childish fights, bullying younger children, swearing, and other normal trouble at school—nothing that merited more than a rebuke from Williams.

When Margaret died when Black was 11 years of age, it was one of the worst possible things imaginable because now he was, again, deprived of a mother. Black was subsequently placed with another foster family in Kinlochleven. He only lived with them a short time because not long after his placement he dragged a young girl into a public bathroom and sexually fondled her. His new foster mother reported the offense to social workers and insisted that Black be placed elsewhere. Black was then sent to the Redding Children's home, a mixed-gender children's home near Falkirk, close to where he was born.

From a young age Black exhibited significant antisocial tendencies, particularly a disturbing awareness of and fascination with sex and women's vaginas. At the age of five he and a girl compared their genitalia. At the age of seven at a school dance he preferred lying on the floor and staring up girls' dresses instead of actually dancing. At the age of eight he took off a neighbor's baby's diaper while he was babysitting to look at her vagina. Despite being heterosexual, Black stated that he would have preferred to have been born female; not that he had any feminine tendencies but he simply hated his penis and would have preferred having a vagina instead. In a prison interview after he was convicted for his heinous crimes, Black confessed to enjoy pushing things up his anus and following his arrest in 1990, police found photographs Black had taken of himself with various unusual objects inserted in his anus. He also confessed to a preoccupation with feces. If one attributed classical Freudian personality psychology, that Black had a tendency to withhold emotion, was oftentimes smelly and messy, and was preoccupied with his anus, then he would be the epitome of an anal personality type.

While in Falkirk, Black was reported as having exposed himself on a number of occasions and, one time, forcibly removing a girl's underwear. At the age of 12 Black made his "first inept attempt at rape." He and two other boys took a girl their age into a field, took off her knickers and lifted her skirt but none were able to "complete the act of penetration." Instead, they touched her vagina and Black admitted that he "forced her to some degree."

After the authorities were called—and had a conference with staff at the Falkirk home—Black was sent to the higher-discipline, all-male Red House in Musselburgh. During his stay there, a male staff member regularly sexually abused him and Black began to solidify his association of sex with dominance and submission.

While in school he developed interests in both swimming and football. Due to poor eyesight he was unable to become a footballer;

however, he was well suited as a lifeguard as he was an excellent swimmer. Further, the sight of young girls in swimsuits fueled his pedophilic fantasies. In fact, 20 years later, when Caroline Hogg was abducted and murdered, her house was en route between the two swimming pools where Black worked as a teenager.

In 1962, when Black was 15, he left the children's home and procured a job as a delivery boy for a butcher. He rented a room in a boys' home in Greenock, near Glasgow, and during this time he admitted to having molested as many as 40 girls while doing his delivery rounds. He claims that when he made a delivery if a young girl was home alone he would sit down and talk to her and then try to touch her.

His first conviction was for lewd and libidinous behavior with a young girl. In 1963, at the age of 17, he approached a seven-year-old girl in a local park and asked her if she would like to accompany him to see some kittens. The naïve girl followed him into a deserted air-raid shelter. He held her by the throat until she lapsed into unconsciousness and he both masturbated over her body and sexually fondled her. She was later found wandering the streets; bleeding, crying, and confused. Black admitted that he didn't know whether she was alive or dead when he left her. Instead of lewd and libidinous behavior, Black should have been charged with and tried for attempted murder. Prior to his 25 June court date, a psychiatric evaluation concluded that this incident was an isolated one and that Black did not need any further treatment.

Black then left Greenock and returned to Grangemouth to start over. After securing employment with a builders' company and renting a room, he finally met his first real girlfriend, Pamela Hodgson. After a physical relationship he fell in love and proposed; however, she broke off the engagement not long after. He was devastated.

In 1966, Black's inappropriate sexual desires resurfaced when he repeatedly molested his landlords' nine-year old granddaughter. While the girl reported it, no charges were filed but Black was asked to leave.

Black returned to his childhood home of Kinlochleven and took a room with a couple who had a seven-year old daughter. Again, he molested the young girl; however, this time the incident was reported and he pled guilty to three counts of indecent assault and was sentenced to a year at Polmont Borstal that was known for rehabilitating the worst of the juvenile criminals. Whereas Black had no problem reiterating all of the aspects of his life and crimes, he has never discussed his time at Borstal, thus leading many to speculate that he was abused during his sentence.

Six months after he was released, Black moved to London and his discovery in child pornography quelled his immediate desire to prey upon young girls. He had discovered that magazines such as *Teenage Sex* and *Lollitots* were clandestinely available, particularly in other countries where pornography laws were less strict such as the Netherlands and he traveled to Amsterdam on several occasions. In fact, when police searched his home after the murders they found over 100 magazines and 50 videotapes depicting child pornography; in addition to Black's own discrete photographs of girls between the ages of eight and 12 he had taken which he kept with his child pornography in a locked suitcase.

Between 1968 and 1970 he held various odd jobs including working as a swimming pool attendant. While here he would oftentimes go underneath the pool, remove the lights, and watch young girls swim. One girl reported that Black had touched her inappropriately and, while no charges were filed, he was fired.

While in London, Black spent considerable time playing darts in pubs—particularly the Three Crowns Pub in Stamford Hill—and became a decent player and a well-known face on the amateur circuit. Many recall Black as a loner who preferred to drink alone irritate others, particularly ladies. During this time Black became acquainted with a Scottish couple named Edward and Kathy Rayson who offered Black lodgings in their empty attic room, which he accepted. He was responsible, albeit reclusive, who—in spite of his poor hygiene—was a model tenant. Although Mrs. Rayson did suspect her lodger of being an avid viewer and reader of pornographic material, neither of the Rayson's thought the material was pedophilic. Black lived with them until his arrest in 1990.

In 1976, after purchasing a white Fiat Transit van, Black secured employment working as a driver for the Hoxton-based Poster Dispatch and Storage, Ltd. that specialized in delivering posters—primarily of music stars—and billboard advertisements. Black would work for PDS for ten years until he was fired due to his constant minor car accidents that cost the company considerable money. Shortly after his dismissal, the company was purchased by two employees who rehired Black because even though he continued to get into accidents, he was a hard worker and was happy to cover for his coworkers by taking the longer runs others didn't care for as they interfered with family commitments. Disturbingly, Black kept a variety of masturbatory tools and girls' clothing which he would don and reenact fantasies in his head; particularly replaying the incident with the seven-year-old girl he had left for dead. When Black committed his first murder it seemed to him like the perfectly natural progression from the fantasy he replayed so frequently.

During his employment, Black became thoroughly familiar with many of London's streets, particularly its minor ones, which would enable him to easily abduct young girls and dump their bodies far from their home without witnesses.

Also during this period, Black changed his appearance multiple time; from shaving his head, growing and/or shaving a beard, and wearing a multitude of different glasses.

The Crimes

Jennifer Cardy, 9

Jennifer Cardy was abducted, sexually assaulted, and murdered on 12 August 1981; a mere two weeks after her ninth birthday. The young girl was last seen by her mother at 1:40 p.m. when she left her house in the County Antrim village of Ballinderry to ride her bicycle to her friend Louise Major's house. When Cardy didn't return home her family telephoned Major's parents where they were informed that their daughter had never even shown up at their house. Cardy's parents called the police and a search for the missing girl was immediately implemented.

Cardy's bicycle—covered with leaves and branches—was discovered an hour later less than one mile from her home. The kickstand of the bicycle was downwards which suggested that, perhaps, Cardy had stopped to talk to someone—likely her abductor—however, there were no witnesses.

Six days after Cardy's disappearance, two hunters found her body in a dam located close to a dual carriageway in Hillsborough, just 15 miles from her home. Her body displayed evident signs of sexual assault and the autopsy concluded that she had died of drowning that was most likely accompanied by ligature strangulation.

Susan Maxwell, 11

On 20 July 1982, 11-year-old Susan Maxwell from Cornhill on Tweed on the English/Scottish border left her home on her bicycle to play tennis in Coldstream. The two-mile route ensured that Maxwell would know most everyone she passed on the way and it was an area where people looked out for each other, especially the children. A number of local witnesses remembered seeing her until she crossed the bridge spanning the River Tweed.

Maxwell's mother Elizabeth reported her daughter missing after she had driven to the tennis courts to pick her up. One of her daughter's friends said that the two girls parted company outside of the Coldstream police station to walk home their separate ways.

The next day a full-scale search began, involving police and search dogs from both sides of the border. At the height of this search, over 300 officers were assigned full time to locate the young girl with activities including canvasing houses in the area and thorough searching every property within the two towns; over 80 square miles of terrain.

While there were no witnesses to the actual abduction, several people described a white van in the area.

An autopsy concluded that Maxwell had died shortly after her abduction; however, the exact date and time of death remains unknown. Maxwell remained in Black's van, whether alive or dead, for 24 hours as his delivery schedule took him into Edinburgh, Dundee, and Glasgow, where he is known to have made his final scheduled delivery at around midnight. The following day, Black returned from Glasgow to London, and discarded Maxwell's body in a copse near the A518 road near Uttoxeter, Staffordshire; 264 miles from where she was abducted.

On 12 August, Maxwell's body was found by Arthur Meadows, a lorry driver, in a ditch near the A518 road at Loxley, near Uttoxeter, in the Midlands; 250 miles from where Maxwell had been abducted. Her body was fully clothed except for her underwear and shoes and her body had been covered with undergrowth. Due to the advanced state of decomposition, she was identified by dental records. The exact date, time, and cause of death could not be determined. What was known, however, was that Maxwell had been bound, her mouth had been gagged with sticking plaster, and her underwear had been removed and neatly folded beneath her head; thus indicating that she had likely been sexually assaulted before her murder; however, the state of the body precluded knowing for sure what, exactly, happened.

Caroline Hogg, 5

Nearly a year later, five-year-Caroline Hogg became Black's youngest known victim. She disappeared while playing in a park near her Beach Lane home in Portobello—a suburb of Edinburgh—in the early evening of 8 July 1983 after begging her mother Annette for "just five more minutes" of playtime. When Hogg had not come home by

7:15 p.m. her parents and brother looked for her. A young boy around Hogg's age said that he had seen her in the company of a man on the nearby promenade, which her mother and brother frantically searched to no avail. Her mother then called the police and reported her young daughter missing.

An intensive search was undertaken which, at that time, was the largest ever in Scottish history. 2,000 local volunteers and 50 members of the infantry regiment Royal Scots Fusiliers searched all over Portobello and neighboring areas; all the way to Edinburgh. The search also attracted considerable local and national media coverage. In fact, by 10 July, the young girl's disappearance was headline news across the entire United Kingdom. Police interviewed the nine known pedophiles who were in Portobello on the night Hogg disappeared but they were all cleared.

Several eyewitnesses had seen an dirty looking, "bald man who wore glasses" watching Hogg as she played before following her to a nearby fairground named Fun City. 14-year-old Jennifer Booth saw Hogg sitting on a bench with this strange man. Booth heard Hogg reply, "Yes please," to some question posed by the man and assumed that they were father and daughter as they walked toward the fairground while holding hands. At Fun City, the man paid 15 pence for Caroline to ride the children's carousel as he watched her. Afterward, she left the fairground in his company. One child witness stated that she had seemed frightened

Not unlike his other victims, Hogg remained in Black's van for at least 24 hours and her exact date, time, and cause of death remains unknown. Black's schedule showed a poster delivery to Glasgow several hours after Hogg's disappearance and he refueled his vehicle in Carlisle in the wee hours of the following morning.

Hogg's naked body was found on 18 July in a ditch off the A444 road between Northampton to Coventry and close to the M1 motorway in Twycross, Leicestershire; 301 miles from where she had been abducted and a mere 24 miles from where Maxwell's body was discovered the previous year.

Due to advanced decomposition, Hogg was identified by her hair band and locket. The exact cause of death was undetermined; however, the entomologist who examined the body asserted that the body could not have been dumped prior to 12 July, thus suggesting that Black may have disposed of her body while making a delivery to Bedworth on the same date. That she was found completely naked also strongly suggested that her murder was sexual.

The following March, a televised reconstruction of Hogg's abduction was broadcast nationally with the hopes of producing further eyewitnesses. Additionally, all parking tickets issued in Edinburgh were examined, tourists as far as Australia were asked to send in rolls of camera and cine film they had taken in Portobello, police sat for weeks by the A444 taking down registration numbers of all vehicles that passed, and investigators searched the homes of all men identified as having been on the promenade that night for "immoral purposes." After the broadcast, Hogg's parents appealed to the public for any anonymous tips to help them find who killed their daughter. Her father said, "You think it can never happen to you, but it has proven time and time again that it can, and it could again if this man isn't caught in the near future."

Sarah Harper, 10

Three years later, ten-year-old Sarah Harper disappeared from Morley, Leeds, at approximately 7:50 p.m. on 26 March 1986, after she left her home on an errand to purchase a loaf of bread from a local market, the K&M, a mere 100 yards from her home. The shop's owner, Mrs. Champaneri confirmed that the girl did, in fact, purchase a loaf of bread and two packages of crisps at approximately 7:55 p.m. and left at 8:05 p.m. She also stated that a balding man entered her store moments later and left when Harper left.

Harper was last seen by two girls walking into an alley leading towards her Brunswick Place home; a shortcut that locals used. When she had not returned by 8:20 p.m., her mother, Jackie, and sister, Claire, briefly searched the surrounding streets before reporting the young girl missing to West Yorkshire Police at approximately 9:00 p.m. Police—as in the other cases—immediately launched an extensive search for the child with over 100 police officers being assigned full-time to look for the young girl. This search involved house-to-house canvases across Morley; the search of over 3,000 properties; distribution of over 10,000 flyers; and the taking of 1,400 witness statements. Additionally, another 200 local volunteers helped search surrounding areas including the search of a reservoir in nearby Tingley by underwater units.

West Yorkshire Police confirmed that a white Transit van had been seen in the area where Harper had been abducted while two suspicious men had been seen in the vicinity near where Harper walked to the store. One of them was a stocky, balding man. Believing that Harper had likely been abducted the police sent a telex to all forces nationwide requesting that they search the areas where other child murder victims had been found.

At a 3 April press conference, Harper's mother Jackie told journalists that she believed her daughter was dead but that the worst thing was not knowing. Appealing to the abductor, Jackie said, "I just want her back, even if she's dead. If someone would just pick up the phone and tell us where the body is." Afterward, Jackie fainted.

On 19 April, while walking his dog, a man named David Moult found Sarah's naked body, gagged and bound, floating in the River Trent near Nottingham, nearly seventy miles from where she was kidnapped.

An autopsy revealed that while the cause of death was drowning, she sustained injuries to her head and neck which likely rendered her unconscious before she was thrown into the water. In addition to being beaten, the evidence demonstrated that Harper had been the victim of a violent and sustained sexual assault—including being sodomized—prior to being tossed into the river. The pathologist described these pre-mortem injuries as "simply terrible." The young victim's father, Terry, Jackie's ex-husband, had to identify his daughter's body and stated that "it was worse than I ever dreamed of."

Investigation and Arrest

By the spring of 1983, whereas many detectives assigned to the inquiry into Maxwell's murder were assigned elsewhere, several detectives did, in fact, remain on the case. When Hogg's body was found in July 1983, Detective Chief Superintendent of Staffordshire Police Dennis Boden held an emergency meeting with senior Staffordshire and Leicestershire detectives to explore the possibility that the same person was responsible for both murders.

Cardy's murder would not be formally linked to the other cases until 2009.

Due to the distance between where the victims were abducted and subsequently found, police suspected that the same person was responsible and that he worked in an occupation that required extensive travel across the United Kingdom, such as a lorry or van driver, or some type of sales representative. Additionally, that both victims were bound and likely subjected to sexual assault—and were clad in white ankle socks when they disappeared—it was presumed that this triggered some sort of fetish response by the perpetrator. It was also decided that due to the circumstantial and geographical nature of the crimes that the perpetrator was likely an opportunist.

Further, since both Maxwell and Hogg were abducted on a Friday, the perpetrator most likely had some sort of delivery or production schedule. After discovery of the bodies, police contacted all transport firms with deliveries in Scotland and the Midlands and all drivers were questioned as to their whereabouts on the dates of the abductions; however, this tactic failed to uncover any potential leads.

Complete cooperation existed between police from the four separate police departments involved in the manhunt. Initially, a satellite incident room that was based in Coldstream coordinated the collective efforts for leads in the Maxwell case while additional incident rooms in Leith and Portobello coordinate the search for evidence in Hogg's case. However, within hours of the discovery of Hogg's body, there was overwhelming consensus that both cases were linked and that they should join efforts with one investigating officer to coordinate all inquiries. Assistant Chief Constable of Northumbia Police Hector Clark was appointed to lead the investigation. Clark established incident rooms in Northumberland and Leith police stations to coordinate all efforts to search for the girls' murderer.

Initially, all information related to both cases was logged with a card-filing system that initially grew to over 500,000 index cards just for the Maxwell case alone. Being familiar with the criticism levied against police during the Yorkshire Ripper case for their being overwhelmed due to the sheer volume of information filed with this type of system, Clark introduced computerized technology into the investigation. Collective use of a computerized database that everyone involved in the investigation could access would improve results. Thus, by December 1986, all of the information related to the three murders (thus far) would be entered into the HOLMES information technology system and additional information would continue to be entered so that police forces nationwide would be able to cross-check all data entered into the system. Initially, detectives looked at individuals who had been convicted of serious sexual crimes against children within the ten years prior to Maxwell's murder in 1982 be further investigated. The list of potential suspects was narrowed to 40,000; however, Black's name never arose as his only conviction was in 1967.

Eventually, this database that was based at the Child Murder Bureau in the West Yorkshire city of Bradford would expand to hold information on over 187,000 individuals; 220,000 vehicles; and 57,000 witness interviews. Much of the information in the database had been obtained through three confidential hotlines established in 1984 by the inquiry team which eventually enabled police to solve numerous other, unrelated crimes, including child abuse offenses.

Several days after Harper's abduction and murder, a witness contacted West Yorkshire Police to inform authorities that on 26 March, at approximately 9:15 p.m., he had seen a white van parked close to the River Soar. A stocky, balding man was standing by the passenger door. Because the River Soar is a tributary to the River Trent and that the vehicle's and man's descriptions were similar to those given by other witnesses, investigators took this account seriously. Furthermore, Black is known to have refueled his van in the Newport Pagnell, Buckinghamshire, the following afternoon; which may suggest that he had taken Harper to the village of Ratcliffe on Soar and had discarded her body in the river either in the evening of the day she was abducted or in the early hours the following morning. Because Harper's abductor likely traveled on the M1 motorway before disposing of her body, investigators from both West Yorkshire and Nottinghamshire Police Departments questioned motorists and staff at all service stations along the M1 motorway between Woolley and Trowell as to whether they might have seen anything unusual on the 26th or 27th of March. Staff at one service station did, in fact, remember a white Transit van that had "seemed out of place" on the evening of 26 March; however, they could not provide a clear description of the driver.

Clark initially did not believe that Harper's murder was connected to Maxwell's and Hogg's due to several dissimilarities; however, in retrospect there were glaring and perhaps more telling similarities. All of the victims were young girls skillfully abducted from public places for sexual purposes and they were driven south and murdered. Further, the three bodies were found within 26 miles of each other in a triangular area known as the Midlands Triangle. Even though Harper's sexual assault appeared to be more vicious than the other two, experts assert that serial killers frequently increase their violence as the murderer gains more confidence and requires more brutality to achieve and maintain arousal. Eight months after Harper was found, Her Majesty's Inspector of Constabulary determined that all three murders were, in fact, linked and that one database be established. Entering all information into a single database took three years and was completed in July 1990.

In 1986, investigators formally requested assistance from the FBI to create a profile of their perpetrator which was completed in January 1988. This profile described the killer as a 30- to 40-year-old white male, likely a loner, who would likely be unkempt in appearance and had received less than 12 years of formal education. He probably lived alone, rented his home, and was in a middle-class neighborhood. Additionally, the profile surmised that the murderer's motives were purely sexual and that he likely had a fixation or obsession with child pornography. Profilers also hypothesized that the killer retained souvenirs from his victims and likely engaged in necrophilia with his victims' bodies shortly after their deaths.

Black was arrested on 14 July 1990, near Stow, Scotland, after snatching six-year-old Mandy Wilson off of the street and bundling her into his van. An alert neighbor, 53-year-old retired postmaster David Herkes, took down the van's registration number and called the police. After a chase, Black was apprehended. The victim was actually the daughter of one of the police officers on the scene and he discovered his daughter in the back of the van, bound and gagged, and stuffed into a sleeping bag. Prior to tying her up, Black had sexually assaulted her. Black was charged with plagium (kidnapping).

When Black's residence was searched, investigators discovered a large collection of child pornography.

Trial and Sentencing

In August 1990, Black was tried and convicted of kidnapping Wilson and given a life sentence. The sentence was based, largely, upon psychiatrists' testimony that Black would continue to pose a great threat to young girls.

Black was still the prime suspect in the murders of Susan Maxwell, Caroline Hogg, and Sarah Harper. Clark decided to interview Black as he was already serving a life sentence for the Wilson kidnapping and Clark mentioned that when he first saw him his gut feeling was that Black was his man. However, instinct and a gut feeling are not good enough for procuring a guilty conviction in a court of law. Black spoke candidly about his prior convictions, about his short relationship with his fiancée, about the sexual abuse he had endured as a child, about his fantasy life, and about his masturbatory practices. When asked specific questions about the three murders he fell silent.

A check of Black's gas receipts and delivery schedules placed him in the vicinity of each girl's abduction and he was charged with all three murders, as well as the attempted kidnapping of a 15-year-old girl who had escaped from the man who tried to drag her into his van in 1988. In this case, on 28 April 1988, 15-year-old Teresa Thornhill had been walking home from the park where she had met friends when Thornhill noticed a blue van stopped ahead. When the driver asked her for help and she denied, he had grabbed her from behind and was taking her to his van. She recalled that he was sweaty and stinky and was able to grab his testicles while screaming. Her friend Andrew, hearing her screams, came to help his friend and chase the assailant away.

Black's murder trial began on 13 April 1994 in front of Judge William MacPherson. Black pled not guilty to the ten charges levied against him which included murder, kidnapping, and preventing the lawful burial of a body. Despite his denial of any guilt, the prosecution was able to place him at each scene and to demonstrate similarities between the three murders and the prior kidnapping for which he had already been convicted and sentenced. His trial lasted five weeks.

On 19 May, the jury found Black guilty of all charges and he was sentenced to life imprisonment with a minimum of 35 years for each charge, to be served concurrently; thus rendering him 82 years old before being eligible for parole—if he were still alive at that time.

On 15 December, Black had been served a formal summons charging him with the murder and sexual assault of Jennifer Cardy and his second murder trial began at Armagh Crown Court on 22 September 2011 before Judge Ronald Weatherup. As he did regarding his other three victims, Black pled not guilty.

Evidence such as gas receipts and delivery schedules demonstrated that Black was in the area at the time Cardy disappeared. This second trial lasted six weeks and on 27 October 2011 he was found guilty of abducting, murdering, and sexually assaulting Cardy. He was given another life sentence.

Aftermath

Black suffered a fatal heart attack while incarcerated at HMP Maghaberry on 12 January 2016, just weeks before he was to be charged with the murder of 13-year-old Genette Tate who had disappeared while delivering newspapers on 19 August 1978 in Aylesbeare, Devon, England.

Senior detectives believe that Black was responsible for eight deaths, in addition to the Tate case; however, 12 other child murders committed across the UK, Ireland, and continental Europe between 1969 and 1987 have also been linked to Black. These include: April Fabb, 13, 8 April 1969, UK; Christine Markham, 9, 21 May 1973, UK; Suzanne Lawrence, 14, 22 July 1979, UK; Patricia Morris, 14, 16 June 1980, UK; Pamela Hastie, 16, 4 November 1981, UK; Mary Boyle, 6, 18 March 1977, Ireland; Silke Garben, 10, 20 June 1985, Germany; Cheryl Morriën, 7, 5 August 1986, Netherlands; Virginie Delmas, 10, 5 May 1987, France; Hemma Devy-Greedharry, 10, 30 May 1987, France; Perrine Vigneron, 7, 3 June 1987, France; and Sabine Dumont, 9, 27 June 1987, France. In all of these cases, Black is known to have been in the area or a white van with a driver who resembled Black was seen.

Prior to his death, Black never admitted culpability in any of the murders for which he was convicted and suspected.

His body was cremated on 29 January and his ashes were discarded at sea.

SICKO JOSEPH DUNCAN

Joseph E. Duncan III

Joseph E. Duncan III is a convicted serial killer, serial rapist, pedophile, stalker, abductor, and sex offender who is currently on death row in Terre Haute, Indiana awaiting his execution date. He was born and raised in Tacoma, Washington on February 25, 1963.

It did not take long for Joseph Duncan to take a wrong direction in life. Supposedly his first sexual encounter was at the age of eight years old with two of his sisters. Four years after that, at the age of twelve, he then sexually assaulted a five-year-old boy. Although this was something he later told a therapist, nothing was confirmed and no chargers were filed. At the tender age of fifteen, he stole a car and led police on a high-speed chase. He ended up crashing into a roadbloc and fled from the vehicle. At the age of sixteen, he kidnapped and forced a fourteen-year-old boy to perform oral sex before raping him (some sources assert that there was another nine year old boy who he raped at gunpoint at some point in time).

He was ultimately charged, pleading guilty to first-degree rape with a firearm and was given a twenty-year sentence. However, it was after these two incidents that he was sentenced to a number of months at Dyslin's Boys Ranch in Tacoma, Washington, a treatment center. While recovering and receiving therapy at the ranch, he told one of his therapists that he had already raped thirteen boys. His modus operandi was to bind them up and repeatedly torture them with sexual assaults.

In 1980, by the time he was seventeen years old he was sentenced to twenty years behind bars for raping a fourteen-year-old boy, again at gunpoint. He broke into a neighbor's house, stole a gun and then forced the young boy into a nearby wooded area with threats of using the gun on him. He sexually assaulted the boy twice before beating him and burning him with cigarettes. Duncan would let the boy go and was later charged with first-degree rape, first-degree burglary and third-degree statutory rape.

While in prison for this rape he was forced to take part in a Sexual Offender Program at Western State Hospital. However, after just under two years in this program his therapist concluded that the therapy was not something that would be helpful to Duncan. He was not willing to adhere to the rules or facility staff; therefore, he was sent back to the state penitentiary where he would serve the rest of his prison sentence. However, some reports state that he was released because he was sneaking out and peeping on other women.

Throughout his sentence he had numerous reviews for protective custody, issues with other inmates, and sexual misconduct. In 1985, he was able to take a job as a teacher's aide at the prison. Unfortunately, he took advantage of that job when he was found sneaking off peeping into homes and masturbating. This particular progress review even mentions that future paroles should bar him from contact with minors. In April of 1988, he took a new job at the prison as a tool crib attendant. By August of that year he was sentenced to ten days of segregation for having a VCR and two x-rated movies in his room. At numerous times throughout his stay in prison from 1988 to 1994 he was put into segregation or was under review for infractions related to sexual misconduct. Many times those who reviewed him said that he needed close supervision and specialized treatment.

He was paroled fourteen years later in 1994 with the understanding that he would have absolutely no contact with children. He went to a halfway house (Interaction Transition House) to try and straighten up his life. He did hold a job as a telemarketer for a little while but would later break parole in 1996 after being caught with marijuana and a firearm. Once again, he was back in jail for thirty days. Joseph Duncan would later have a parole revocation hearing to determine whether he should stay in jail or be released. Dr. Wacksman testified on his behalf, but the board denied his request. Duncan went back to prison until July of 2000. Upon his release he traveled up to Washington for a visit with his mother and then to Fargo, North Dakota for a visit with Dr. Wacksman.

What he did during the few years between 2000 until the 2005 murders and kidnapping of Mark McKenzie and the Groene's is not completely known and probably never will be. Although, he did confessed to some additional crimes while in jail for the 2005 murders of Mark McKenzie and the Groene's, there are probably several more that investigators will never know about. The 2005 murders and kidnapping as well as several other crimes are outlined below.

Sammiejo White and Carmen Cubias

After Joseph Duncan's thirty days in jail he was staying a few blocks from a motel that Sammiejo White and Carmen Cubias were staying. Both the eleven year old, Sammiejo, and nine year old, Carmen, went missing from the motel on July 6, 1996. The two sisters were leaving the motel late in the evening to go get cigarettes for their older brother.

They never returned.

It was not uncommon for these children to be out so late. In fact, there were several other siblings in this household and they were all known in the neighborhood.

Police never knew if the girls ran away or were victims of a crime. However, their bodies were found two years later on February 10, 1998 in Bothell, Washington. It was determined that they were probably killed shortly after being kidnapped. The case was denoted a cold case for years until August of 2005 when Joseph Duncan provided police with details of what happened to the two girls in 1996. Although he never actually confessed, he did give enough specific details of what happened to the girls that made for an easy confession. An eyewitness later confirmed that she saw Joseph Duncan and a girl that looked like Carmen Cubias at a grocery store. The girl seemed frightened from what the witness said. This was one of Duncan's signature moves (keeping victims alive for a period of time). The details from each of his cases are very similar making it easier to link past cases and crimes to Duncan.

Anthony Martinez

Joseph Duncan was also implicated in a 1997 case involving a ten-year-old boy in California. On April 4, 1997 an unknown man approached Anthony Martinez at his home in Beaumont, California. He and some of his friends were playing football in his front yard when the man asked for help finding his cat. All of the boys refused his help the strange man, but the man became enraged and grabbed one of the boys. He used a knife to scare the boy and the other kids. He put the child who was later identified as Anthony Martinez in his vehicle and fled the scene.

On April 19, 2005 Anthony Martinez's body was found in Indio naked and bound. An autopsy revealed that Anthony had been brutally sexually assaulted. Although there was duct tape used to bind Anthony and a partial fingerprint from that tape, the case did go cold. It was not until after the 2005 Idaho murder that Joseph Duncan was tied to the Martinez case. Once the Federal Bureau of Investigations (FBI) started tying similarities together, it become obvious that Joseph Duncan was involved. Authorities tested his fingerprints against the one found on the tape and it was a confirmed match.

After the 2005 kidnapping and murders of the Groene and McKenzie family, Joseph Duncan did confess to the murder of Anthony Martinez; therefore, in April of 2011 Duncan plead guilty to the murder of Antony Martinez and received two consecutive life sentences for his death.

Duncan was then sentenced to life in prison in 2011 for the murder of Anthony Martinez.

2005 Idaho Murders

The 2005 killing and kidnapping spree of Joseph Duncan began because of his bond release from a Minnesota jail. First, it is important to note that he was in jail because of the suspected molestation of two boys. In March of 2005, he was charged with the July 3, 2004 molestation of two boys at a playground in Detroit Lakes, Minnesota. His bond was for about $15,000 and after being released from jail he skipped his bond. He began making plans to leave the state immediately.

He was able to convince a businessman, Joe Crary, to pay his $15,000 bond (with a personal check). Apparently they had a romantic relationship and Joseph Duncan did an outstanding job of making it seem like he was a misunderstood man with the discipline to turn his life around. Little did Joe Crary know what was coming next would be one of the worst crimes in Idaho history.

Joseph Duncan meticulously planned his crime, stopping to pick up tools at a Walmart. He bought night vision goggles, a video camera, a shotgun, shells, and a claw hammer. After about two weeks, he decided it was time to leave the state of Minnesota. He rented a red Jeep Grand Cherokee in St. Paul, Minnesota and traveled out of state. He went through Missouri then entered Idaho with plans to go on a killing rampage.

Duncan stole license places off of another vehicle and placed them on the red Jeep Cherokee to avoid detection and capture. He knew that at some point the vehicle he rented would be reported as stolen. He drove up Interstate 90 towards Coeur d'Alene, Idaho. He made landfall there roughly five weeks after his hearing for sexually assaulting a six-year-old boy. Authorities do not know exactly why he stopped in Coeur d'Alene, Idaho, possibly for gas or food, but he did. He located the Groene and McKenzie home in a secluded area, not far off the frontage road.

Duncan saw Shasta Groene (eight years old) and her brother, Dylan (nine years old), playing in the front yard of the house. It was the kind of neighborhood where people felt confident in letting thier children play outside at will. Children played at the park, rode their bikes and came and went from house to house without a care in the world. A world that didn't have the likes of Joseph Duncan until now.

The Groene and McKenzie home was one of the first houses you see when one enters the neighborhood, but also very secluded with trees. The house was off the frontage road a ways, but positioned in a way that it was the first one available in case of an emergency. Many strangers had stopped by before if there was a problem and they needed help. The Groene and McKenzie family never turned anyone away. They were always willing to help someone in needed.

It is believed that Joseph Duncan was intrigued by the children and the ease of the community that this felt like the right time and the right family to attack. He used a few days to survey the family and perform reconnaissance prior to confronting them. May 15th, 2005 was the last time anyone saw Mark McKenzie, Brenda Groene and Slade Groene alive. The family had been to a large barbeque with other neighbors that evening before heading home.

Authorities were alerted on Monday, May 16, 2005, when a neighbor went by the residence to pay Slade for mowing his grass the day before. The neighbor said that the house was very quiet, there were no lights on in the house, but both vehicles were home with car doors left open. It seemed odd and it was appropriate that authorities check it out. It is also important to note that the same neighbor had seen a white pick up at the house earlier in the day. Apparently that neighbor was the one that called authorities to report the suspicious activity earlier in the day

The Kootenai County Sheriff's Department sent deputies to check out the house and check on the family. After surveying the outside of the house, deputies decided to gain access to the house to check on the wellness of the homeowners.

Upon entering the house from the backyard, they found two bodies in the kitchen area that were duct taped and zip tied. Both had been brutally killed either by blunt force trauma to the head or a gunshot wound. One was a male and the other was a female. Deputies also found an additional victim in the living room, also bound by duct tape and zip tied. Again, the third victim had blunt force trauma to the head or a gunshot wound. After investigating the rest of the house, it was determined that the three victims were Mark McKenzie, his girlfriend Brenda Groene, and her son, thirteen year-old Slade Groene. Brenda's younger children, Shasta Groene (eight years old) and Dylan Groene (nine years old), were nowhere to be found.

At this point, the case then turned to the two missing children. Search teams gathered to cover terrain around the Groene and McKenzie home and Lake Coeur d'Alene. The search team included deputies with trained search dogs, helicopters, volunteers on foot, as well as the Federal Bureau of Investigation (FBI). An Amber Alert was issued with pictures and descriptions to ensure as many people as possible knew about the two missing children. Authorities also set up an emergency tip line that allowed citizens to call in tips if they had any information about the two missing children. Within the first twelve hours, the police had over 150 calls. Volunteers helped take calls and sift through the information to determine what might be a valuable lead or not. Some tips included information about where the children's favorite play spots were, possible sightings, etc. Unfortunately, the tips did not generate many useful leads and most did not pan out. This case quickly became the largest in Kootenai County history and even generated an FBI reward of $100,000. However, the case was not generating any traction. The case was growing cold every day. America's Most Wanted even ran a special on May 21, 2005 to help generate new leads to find the children. Nine new tips came in, but none of them panned out either.

However, two days prior to the America's Most Wanted TV special, the children's biological father gave a heartfelt plea to release his children. During that time frame, a sporting goods store own in Bonners Ferry, Idaho called in to the police department with a huge tip. He told deputies that a man with two children fitting Shasta and Dylan's descriptions came into the store asking for directions to Montana. He said that they left in a white van with Washington state license plates. Unfortunately, even after notifying Idaho State Police there were no signs of the van or the children.

During this time, investigators were still trying to determine the cause of the deaths of Brenda, Mark and Slade. Several different scenarios were being suggested for motive, especially after toxicology results determined that both Brenda and Mark had THC and methamphetamines in their system at the time of their death. First, investigators tried to determine if it was one person or more that killed the family. Since they were bound, investigators thought there may have been more than one person involved. Some ideas included a drug deal gone bad, gang killings, or something similar. The motive for the killings and the kidnappings were dumbfounding to investigators.

Time was slipping away from authorities making this investigation harder and harder on everyone involved. However, on July 2nd at 1:30 in the morning the same red Jeep Cherokee that Joseph Duncan had rented just after his release from jail showed up at a local Denny's in Coeur d'Alene. A middle aged man and a little girl matching the description of Shasta walked into the restaurant together. Two men outside the restaurant and a waitress inside the restaurant recognized little Shasta. They quietly notified the manager of the Denny's who called 911. Three police cars showed up about ten minutes after the middle-aged man and little Shasta arrived at Denny's.

Joseph Duncan was arrested and Shasta was rescued. Unfortunately, Dylan was not found in the Jeep Cherokee.

After Shasta was rescued, police were able to put a better timeline together. Joseph Duncan broke into the Groene and McKenzie home in the middle of the night on July 5, 2005. Shasta's mother, Brenda, woke up her and carried her into the living room where she encountered Joseph Duncan. Duncan took Shasta and Dylan to a white truck outside. He placed them into the truck where they did not witness the brutal murders of Mark, Brenda and Slade. After Duncan murdered the rest of the family, he took Shasta and Dylan to a remote location where the Jeep Cherokee was hidden. He used a white truck to transport the kids to the Jeep Cherokee. He then moved the children to the other vehicle and took off for Montana. The three of them stayed in two separate campsites in Montana for six weeks where Joseph Duncan repeatedly raped and sexually abused both Shasta and her brother, Dylan.

Shasta told investigators that Duncan told her in vivid detail how he killed her family and how he watched them for several days prior to breaking into their home. He also told her the he sexually assaulted her other brother Slade. She was able to give enough details about their campsite that investigators were also able to locate the place where Duncan kept them, which ultimately led to the discovery of Dylan's remains.

Joseph Duncan was originally charged with two counts of first-degree kidnapping in Idaho, which warrants death, or life in prison. With evidence linking him to the Groene and McKenzie murders, he was also charged with three counts of first-degree murder, which means that Joseph Duncan would serve three consecutive life sentences. Although after recovering Dylan's body it was determined the little boy was shot to death and burned to cover up evidence. With this discovery, an additional charge of murder was added. At this point, Duncan also chooses to waive his right to appeal the death sentences.

Joseph Duncan is currently on death row awaiting his execution date for these murders.

Dr. Richard Wacksman

Dr. Richard Wacksman testified on behalf of Joseph Duncan during his parole violation hearing in 1997. He told the court that Duncan was no longer a harm or danger to society and that he was a reformed citizen. He also told the court that Joseph Duncan could come live with him while he got back on his feet. Evidentially, Dr. Wacksman had helped quite a few felons get back on their feet in the past. The court clearly did not believe Duncan was ready for society yet and sent him back to prison for three more years until 2000. Then on July 21, 2000, Duncan moved to Fargo, North Dakota. Dr. Wacksman helped Duncan out by giving him money, a place to stay, a car, and even money for tuition to North Dakota State University.

Apparently, the two had a romantic relationship, even though Dr. Wacksman was married with children. The two met in the mid-90's at a gay bar in San Francisco. Eventually Dr. Wacksman moved to Florida, which Duncan did visit quite often for scuba diving trips. The two men stayed in heavy contact until Dr. Wacksman realized that Joseph Duncan was manipulating him every step of the way.

Other Potential Victims

Other possible victims of Joseph Duncan include Steven Earl Kraft Jr., Russell Turcotte, Leanne "Beaner" Warner, Justin Phillip Edwards and other molestation victims.

Steven Earl Kraft, Jr., a twelve year-old boy took his two dogs out for an evening walk in Benton Harbor, Michigan on February 15, 2001. He was last seen leaving around 7:00 pm with both dogs, but only one dog came back. That dog led his parents to a local pond, but there was nothing there to reflect that Steven Kraft, Jr. had been there. Although the other dog, a puppy, was later found near a creek. To this date, the case still remains unsolved and is a cold case, but it is suspected that Joseph Duncan is somehow involved in the kidnapping and possible murder of this young teen.

Russell Turcotte, a nineteen year-old boy was last heard from by his mother. He contacted her for money, needing a bus ticket home. Last seen in Grand Folks, North Dakota on July 12, 2002 after a weekend with friends. His remains were found at Devils Lake about ninety miles east of the truck stop. Surveillance cameras at the truck stop have both Russel Turcotte and Joseph Duncan at the truck stop within hours of each other. The probable story is that Duncan picked up a hitch hiking Russell Turcotte to or from the truck strop. Duncan most likely took Russell to a remote location, raped him and then killed him just like his other signature cases. Russell's body was not found until November of 2002. One of the biggest reasons that Joseph Duncan is a suspect in this case, besides being seen at the truck stop, is the fact that Russell Turcotte's head was crushed in much the same manner as Duncan's prior victims have been (Sammiejo White, Carmen Cubias, Anthony Martinez, Mark McKenzie and Slade Groene). The similarities in the cases are too coincidental not to suspect Joseph Duncan as a possibility.

Leanne "Beaner" Warner was last seen on June 14, 2003. Beaner was a nickname her grandfather affectionately gave her. She was only five years old at the time she went missing. Beaner headed over to a friend's house that evening, but the family was out at the time of her arrival. Two eyewitness neighbors stated they did see little Beaner around 5:00 pm. When Beaner did not show back up from her friend's house her parents Chris and Kaelin Warner became worried. They finally contacted police around 9:00 pm after the parents went looking themselves. The family lived in a small town of Chisholm, Minnesota. The town is home to roughly 5,000 people and was considered a safe community. The police initially thought maybe she got lost; there were no leads that made them think an abduction had occurred. Although search dogs did find her scent at Longyear Lake as well as her footprints, no other evidence was uncovered. She was also at the lake earlier in the day with her mother, so it was hard to determine if this was relevant or not. However, it is important to note that Joseph Duncan would make frequent trips to this area for scuba diving trips. On this particular day he went skydiving with friends near West Fargo, North Dakota where he has pictures and videos that puts him close to the location. In Duncan's video, he discusses his scuba diving trip that he had taken in the Chisholm area within a few days of Beaner's disappearance. The video also includes tons of footage of children running and playing in an airport. A little random for someone to have children they do not know on their video. In his blog he also talks about this crime in detail. Unfortunately, Beaner's case is still cold and he has never confessed to her crime. He is still a prime suspect.

Justin Phillip Harris was last seen at his group home in Casper, Wyoming. The morning that the staff found him missing his bed was made so that it looked like someone was still sleeping in it. It is not likely that Justin could do this because he was mentally disabled with the mind of a six year old. There is nothing that ties Duncan to this disappearance, but his blog states that he went skiing over that weekend alone. It is believed that he is involved somehow.

Joseph Duncan is also suspected in numerous other molestations throughout his years out of prison.

Conclusion

Joseph E. Duncan III is a sick individual that should have been locked away for life many, many, years ago. He has repeatedly committed crimes that make it obvious he is not fit for society and a nuisance to everyone he comes into contact with. He is a serial killer and sex offender that is a danger to society. The horrendous acts he has committed are beyond comprehension and unthinkable to even those in law enforcement.

Currently, his attorneys continue to file appeals on his behalf to overturn his death sentences (against his will by the way). The latest attempt was in March of 2015 with his attorneys fighting to overrule that he was mentally competent when he waived his right to appeal the 2005 murder and kidnapping of nine year old, Anthony Martinez. This has yet to be resolved, so Joseph Duncan is still on death row awaiting execution by lethal injection.

Duncan is still expressing his life and feelings on his blog "The Fifth Nail Exposed: Confessions". The site is broken down into categories: Introductions, Letters, Reflections, Inquiry, Confessions, Dreams,

Chronicles and Books. He basically details vivid memories from his childhood to specific crimes he has committed.

THE BONDAGE MURDERS : THE TRUE STORY OF SHIRLEY WITHERS

MARY MAXWELL

Shirley Withers and Peter Shellard looked to be a mismatched couple.

Shellard was a multi-millionaire dollar real estate mogul and high-end car dealer. Logic would dictate that he would date much younger women, seducing aspiring actresses and models with his wealth. But Shirley was anything but a supermodel. She was an ordinary looking bookkeeper, thirty-three-years-old, and bit on the frumpy side.

"He was a hot shot," forensic psychologist Paula Orange said. "An eccentric hotshot but still very well-to-do. He would strut around town wearing fancy suits with matching socks but wear sandals over them. Shirley, on the other hand, was very unassuming. She looked like the typical cubicle drone. A little overweight and plain looking. Nothing sexy about her."

Their relationship, however, would be one of the biggest firestorms of sex, murder, and drugs in Australian history.

BEGINNINGS

Shirley was born in New Delhi, India in 1966. She immigrated with her family to Australia when she was a child. She married young and had two sons with her first husband. By 2000, she would be divorced and immediately be on the market for a new beau.

Enter Peter Shellard.

Peter, born in 1949, touted himself as a self-made millionaire although he had a benefactor in an older, maternal figure in Vera Moore.

He didn't finish high school, dropping out to obtain his real estate agent's license at night. Once he acquired that, he began leveraging properties around the Brighton area eventually making a fortune in addition to buying a high-end car dealership.

He called his company "Peter Shellard Real Estate" and then used that money to help finance a deal where he took control over Kellow-Falkiner Motors. He juggled both real estate as well as used Rolls-Royce and Bentley parts.

Shellard's businesses continued to flourish. He purchased many companies as well as commercial and rental properties.

"He hung around some heavy hitters in his area," Orange said. "People who could buy Rolls Royces without batting an eye."

Shellard would purchase the Rosecraddock Place in North Caulfield, a regal mansion which would later sell for over $7 million upon his death. As his wealth grew, he began collecting high-end cars which included a 1923 Rolls-Royce, a 1951 Rolls-Royce Silver Dawn, and a Mercedez-Benz 450SL convertible.

AN ECCENTRIC NUT

Shellard did have mental issues, however, suffering from bipolar disorder.

"His mansion was filled with all kinds of knick-knacks," Orange said. "Stuff that seemed disconnected and junky. But he was bipolar and people with that ailment tend to have different eccentricities. His was to hoard stuff among other things."

Shellard was reported to be a recluse, sheltering himself from the outside world as he became more wealthy. He had a barbed wire fence built high around the mansion but it served more to keep him in then keeping people out. His neighbors would rarely see him outside the compound unless he was walking his dogs. He also had ponies and kept an area for beehives. Neighbors complained about the bees and the city had the hives destroyed. Shellard would later file suit and demand that he have the remains of his dead bees returned.

Shellard would treat other homeowners as if they were peasants and would come and go on their private grounds as he pleased. One neighbor reported that Shellard came into their backyard and began sifting through their garden tools. Another complained that Shellard would park one of his Rolls-Royces in their personal garage. Shellard was informed to remove the vehicle after which he became enraged and began to tear apart the garage. He would then be sued for the action and was forced to pay almost $2000 in damages.

"Obviously, he walked around as if he had a sense of entitlement," Orange said. "Definitely a narcissistic sociopath but he could turn on the charm when he wanted. It all depended on what he wanted. When he was trying to make a sale, he could charm you. When he was doing something stupid and you called him on it, that is when he went berserk."

Town councilwoman Veronika Martens had plenty of bizarre dealings with Shellard as well. On one occasion, Shellard chopped down some cypress trees on his property and began burning the branches. Neighbors called to complain and firefighters came down to extinguish the flames.

Enraged, Shellard began attacking the firefighters and cut through the fire hoses with an ax.

Later, Shellard would be caught breaking into Caulfield Town Hall by climbing in through the roof. He would also come into the building unannounced, enter unoccupied offices and begin making phone calls.

"Shellard was an aggressive, anti-government guy," Orange said. "He went so far as to try to have his mansion designated as a religious place in order to avoid taxes. The judge got a good laugh at that one. The religion of what? Nutty behavior?"

Angered that his request was denied, he began making plans to tear down the mansion and divide up the land. But legal maneuverings blocked him from doing that as city council members had his mansion placed on the Historic Buildings Council, giving it legal protection.

A SADO-MASOCHIST

A ladies man, Shellard would marry twice. He had three daughters, Jenny, Clare and Sarah, before divorcing his second wife Elizabeth in 1994.

Shellard really did not have any bad habits that than his eccentricities as he abstained from both alcohol and smoking. He did have one fetish, however, and that was sadomasochism.

Shellard would go to clubs and participate in bondage sessions, preferring visits to the Hellfire Club in Brighton. Once there, he would "dress up in a full range of leather outfits and had belts with studs."

Shellard would go to the Hellfire Club to be whipped.

"He told me initially that his pain threshold was very low," Shellard's friend Christine Smith said. "And after a number of visits his tolerance for pain increased to the point where he really liked what was occurring. He found it very erotic."

By 2001, he was looking for a new partner and found one in Shirley Withers.

"Initially mum and I thought Shirley was a bit odd," Jenny, Shellard's eldest daughter recalled. "She would never look you in the eye. She was always very kind, though."

ENTER SHIRLEY WITHERS

Opposites attract, and Shellard soon began wooing Shirley with his luxurious lifestyle. He brought her numerous gifts, jewelry, and clothing.

"I'll bankroll all your dreams," he teased.

Shirley took him up on the offer, expressing her desire to run her own clothing boutique.

"Shellard did anything and everything for Shirley," forensic psychologist Paula Orange said. "He bought her everything she asked for evening financing her 'dream' of running a boutique store in a prestigious area of Brighton. Never mind the fact that Shirley had no business experience. Shellard believed he had money to burn."

"You can't be serious?" Shirley gushed when Peter told her he would buy her a clothing company.

"What are you going to call it?" Shellard asked, smiling.

"God," Shirley said. "God. I don't know. How about Suzette? Suzette Boutique?"

"Suzette Boutique!" Shellard laughed aloud as Shirley hugged him in appreciation.

Shellard made all the arrangements for Shirley to run the store. He had it designed and built to her specifications.

Shirley would have all of the brand name fashions in her store. She loaded the shelves with Marianna Hardwick, Charlie Brown, and Lisa Ho.

Shellard had one caveat and that was having his eldest daughter, Jenny, work in the boutique. Jenny herself, however, had a less than flattering impression of both Shirley and her attempts to run a business.

"My first impression when I started working there was that it was just a mess," Jenny said. "I couldn't understand how Shirley kept paying us every week. I had seen invoices totaling thousands of dollars and wondered where Shirley was getting the money. Shirley would just continuously buy stock for the business and for herself. She definitely had a problem with spending money."

Shellard did not stop at just buying Shirley her own boutique.

He bought her a house.

"It was a bit of an odd arrangement," Orange said. "They had separate living quarters. Shellard wanted his own house to himself and would visit Shirley for coital purposes."

Shellard displayed further bad judgment when he allowed Shirley to be put in charge of the accounting of his car dealership.

"He figured she was a bookkeeper," Orange said. "She must know what she's doing."

Shellard's naivete didn't end there as he allowed Shirley access to his property accounts in addition to becoming a signatory on his car dealership.

What Shellard didn't take into account was that Shirley was not a person he could trust nor did she know what she was doing.

Her boutique began to fail. She had purchased too much product and the few items that did sell would not have a high enough margin. Being a marginal business person, she continued to purchase inventory despite not generating any revenue.

The store began losing money. Lost of it.

So Shirley took it upon herself to begin stealing from Shellard's dealership. She would write checks to herself in upwards of $10,000. Shellard began noticing the discrepancies and called in his accountant.

After checking the books, the two realized that Shirley stole over $900,000, a significant amount of Shellard's wealth.

NO CURE FOR A SPENDAHOLIC

Shellard owned over eleven properties and his total net worth looked to be about $10-15 million.

By the time Shellard had finally got wind of Shirley's financial doings, she had amassed over $43,000 in credit card debt while her store was almost $275,000 in the red.

"She simply had no idea what she was doing," Orange said. "She spent and spent and spent."

To top it off, she had siphoned nearly a million dollars from the dealership account, funding the boutique and her own shopping sprees.

"She's robbing you blind," the accountant said. "You should go to the police."

"I'll take care of it," Shellard said. "Let me handle it."

Shellard began to take action. He informed his bank that he wanted Shirley removed as the signatory for his automotive dealership. Then he called a meeting with his friend, Eugene Hand and his lawyer Stuart Winston

"She's ripping me off," Shellard said. "The bitch is robbing me blind. She shuttled over $150,000 into her own account."

"You need to call the police," Winston said.

"I'm going to sell her house," Shellard said. "Fuck her. I need to recoup that loss."

Shellard then confronted Shirley about stealing his money. He was livid, demanding to know what she had been doing.

"He obviously felt betrayed," Orange said. "He was crazier than a shithouse rat, but let's face it, the guy had been good to her. He bought her everything she wanted and let her join him in this decadent lifestyle. But it wasn't good enough for her. She stole his credit cards. Wrote checks in his name payable to her."

Shirley didn't feel remorse at the dressing down by Shellard. She just didn't want the gravy train to leave.

THAT MONEY AIN'T GOING NOWHERE

Shirley began looking for a solution. She noticed a scraggly, down and out woman visiting her boutique often and a light bulb went on her head.

The woman was named Sophia.

Sensing she was a person with some wrong side of the street connections, Shirley saw Sophia and her boyfriend Stanley as "useful idiots" in a plot to kill her husband. They were low-level drug dealers willing to do anything for a buck.

Even if it included murder.

"Shirley gave them a song and dance about how she was an abused spouse," Orange said. "She told the two junkies that she had to endure nightly beatings and rapes. How Shellard would tie her up and have his way with her."

Sophia and Stanley, despite being heroin addicts and petty criminals, felt moral indignation.

Then Shirley waved a few thousand dollars in their face and they were willing to do whatever she asked.

On May 6th, 2005, Shirley lead the two junkies into Shellard's home.

"He's sound asleep in his bed until Shirley attacks him, placing a pillow case over his head," Orange said. "The two junkies hold Shellard down but he begins to fight. He struggles with Sophia and bites her finger. The junkie screams and takes some kind of heavy object from the bedside table and smashes Shellard over the head with it."

Shellard is knocked unconscious but that is when Shirley goes to work.

She takes a needle and injects him with heroin as she wants to make everything look like an overdose.

Then they pulled down his pants.

"Shellard is starting to come to," Orange said. "Then they shove a suppository up his rectum. Oxycontin. This coupled with the heroin is a powerful mix as he has a heart condition. A knock on the head, a shot of heroin and some Oxycontin shoved up his ass killed the man."

Peter is left for dead as Shirley lets some time pass before she calls the police.

A BAD ACTRESS AND A PAIR OF BUNGLING CRIMINALS

Shirley then conjures up her best Meryl Streep act as she calls the police and tells them that she has found Shellard dead on the floor.

"He was into rough sex," she blubbered. "I don't know who could have done this to him."

Police arrived and found the dead Shellard with a towel covering his genitals. His ankles were handcuffed and he was wearing a mouth gag. He also had dog leads, electrical cords and ropes tied around him.

Unfortunately for Shirley, however, the two junkies she hired were not exactly professionals.

A fingerprint sweep led police to Sophia.

Her print had been found on a hallway telephone. They would also find her DNA on a partially smoked cigarette in the kitchen.

The police would track down Sophia as well as her junkie boyfriend. They both confessed to the crime.

"I did it," Stanley said the moment he took a seat in the interrogation room. "Well, I should say that I helped them do it. Shirley drove me and Sophia to the mansion. She wanted him tied up because he had forced her to do bondage with him. Bondage! The dude had frozen all her accounts and was trying to sell her house behind her back. She told him that she wanted to sign some papers so that she could get her house back."

Stanley described the evening of the killing as a casual night on the town. He stated that Shirley took Sophia and himself to a hotel for some gambling.

"We played the poker machines," Stanley told the police. "Then we got some heroin and went to the mansion. Shirley had a syringe of heroin. She went into his bedroom and stuck him with it."

Shellard's daughters, all decent young women, were in shock at what happened to her father. Shirley took it upon herself to try and comfort Jenny but didn't mince words about the kind of man he was.

"Your father was into bondage," Shirley said to her after she tried to sell the police on the fact that Shellard's death was likely due to rough sex. "We never hurt each other, though."

"After my dad died, I confided in Shirley for support," Jenny said. "I thought that she would be the only one who could possibly understand the pain I was going through because she was going through it too."

Shirley didn't know that while she was talking daily on the phone with Jenny, the police had her phone tapped.

They would find out that Shirley was calling around asking for a hitman.

Setting up a sting, they assigned an undercover officer for the operation.

A HITMAN COMETH

Shirley made it known that she was looking for someone to "off" both Sophia and Stanley, thereby getting rid of her only witnesses.

An undercover officer, code-named "Victor" called Shirley and set up four meetings.

"Can you get me pictures of them?" Victor asked.

"No," Shirley said. "But I can get you their address."

"What do they do for a living?"

"They don't 'do' anything," Shirley scoffed. "They're fucking junkies. They sit around all day and shoot heroin."

"Why do you want them killed?"

"They were responsible for killing my husband," Shirley said. "I want them both taken care of."

"It will cost you ten thousand dollars," Victor said. "I need three grand up front. Down payment."

"No problem."

"I need you to get as specific as you can," the hitman said. "Do you want it to be quick or do you want them to suffer?"

"Yes," Shirley said, her eyes cold.

"But do you want them dead?" the hitman asked again. "Or in a wheelchair for the rest of their lives?"

"I want them both dead," Shirley said with finality. "Dead."

Shirley would be arrested and charged with Shellard's murder while the two junkies would receive six years in jail for manslaughter.

In 2007, however, Shirley would elect to go to trial. In her appeal, she somehow convinced the judge that she didn't mean to kill Shellard. She only meant to teach him a lesson.

Shirley would be sentenced to thirteen years in prison which could be lessened to nine years with good behavior.

At the time of this writing, Shirley has become eligible for parole.

A FINAL BETRAYAL

The story took another turn for the bizarre when trustees of Vera Moore's estate would claim that millions of dollars that Moore gave Shellard were meant as a loan and not a gift.

They argued that it should be repaid.

Moore had died eight years prior to Shellard being murdered. He had been a good friend of her son, Kenneth, who died in a car crash in 1972.

Moore then took a shine to the young Shellard, treating him as if he were her own son.

She would give him her son's Waring Bros Tourer Rolls-Royce. In return, Shellard would keep the elderly widow company. He would take her out of her suburban nursing home and drive her around in the Rolls-Royce while they would go out for tea.

"By all accounts," Orange said. "He seemed to have been good to her. Like a son. He was soon given the power of attorney for her and looked after her financial affairs."

Shellard would purchase the Rosecraddock mansion in 1984 for $1.4 million. This was done with Moore's money as the title was split between her company, Brenchley Gardens, and Shellard's company then called "Landro."

Shellard would always seem to have bad luck with women, not only while alive but in death as well as even the attorneys for his mother figure in Vera Moore would turn on him.

GARY GILMORE, SERIAL KILLER

SARAH THOMPSON

McCamey, Texas. A town of less than two thousand people, out in the scorching Texas desert, where downtown is a stretch of black road with marginally more buildings on either side. McCamey is the type of town that lies, more or less, entirely forgotten by the rest of the United States, down in the deep heat of Texas. It was in McCamey, in 1940, that Gary Mark Gilmore was born. Gilmore would have, perhaps, gone one to live and die a completely unnoticed life if circumstances had been different. As it stands, Gary Mark Gilmore would gain fame through his life for being the first person sentenced to death in the United States in nearly ten years for the crimes that he committed.

On December 4th, in 1940, Frank and Bessie Gilmore became the parents of their second son, Gary Mark Gilmore. Frank and Bessie were married on a whim, and Frank was said to have other wives and families that he otherwise ignored. Bessie was a Mormon from Provo, Utah, but she had been outcast by her community. Bessie and Frank met and married in California, but the both of them eventually moved to McCamey, Texas, where Gary Mark had been born. Gilmore would have three brothers: Frank Jr., Gaylen and Mikal Gilmore. It was in McCamey that Frank and Bessie were living with their first son Frank Jr., and existing under the false name of "Coffman" in order to escape detection from law enforcement. When he was born, Gary Mark Gilmore had been given the name Faye Robert Coffman - Faye, named after Frank Gilmore Sr.'s mother, Fay.

However, the name Faye Robert didn't stick. His mother, Bessie, decided to change it to Gary Mark Gilmore after they left Texas. Moving wasn't uncommon for the Gilmore family. Gary spent most of his childhood moving from city to city throughout most of the Western United States, along with this three brothers and his parents. Frank Gilmore supported the family during this time with the sale of fraudulent magazine subscriptions. Gary's relationship with his father was rocky, as was the rest of the family's relationship with Frank Gilmore, Sr. He was described as a man with a quick temper, and who was easily angered. He was also a strict father, and one to dole out corporal punishment when and if he saw fit. Frank often did not need a reason to beat his sons, and would routinely whip them with a razor strop, belt or whip.

Frank Gilmore, Sr. did not only take out his anger and violence on his sons. Though this was less frequent, he would also take to beating Bessie. The relationship between Frank and Bessie was also volatile. Gary grew up in a household in which his parents would often take to screaming at one another, and verbally abusing one another with insults and digs at each other's religions. Bessie would even threatened to kill Frank Sr. some nights. The two parental figures of the household were constantly at one another's throats, and it was the source of a lot of distress and frustration and turmoil within the Gilmore family.

Exposure to violence between his mother and father and the crimes of his father did nothing for Gary's disposition. While his other brothers seemed to escape the thrall of their household unscathed, Gary wasn't so lucky. There's no telling what a calmer household would have done for Gary, and if his rocky home life was the root cause for the crimes he would commit and the path he would soon begin to take in life.

Despite the Gilmore family's nomadic lifestyle for the greater part of Gary's children, they finally settled down in Portland, Oregon in the year 1952. Gary was twelve at the time, and like most twelve year olds, he was starting to stretch his legs and discover some semblance of independence and self-identity. During his adolescence, Gary was incredibly intelligent. He tested an IQ score of 133, and throughout his schooling career he tested and scored well on both aptitude and achievement tests. Gary even showed an incredible ability for artistic talent. He was on the entirely right track to being a successful student and graduating from school.

Unfortunately, Gary did not continue down this path. He was in the ninth grade when he decided to drop out of high school. It was then that Gary became caught up in petty crimes, and took to anti-social behaviors. After he dropped out of high school, Gary ran away from home with a friend. They traveled from Oregon all the way down to Texas. There they stayed for several months before finally returning back to Portland. It was at 14 that he finally managed to succumb to his first arrest. He had started a car theft ring with some friends. Rather than put him in jail, law enforcement released him back to his father and all Gary received from police was a slap on the wrist and a warning to keep in line.

Gary didn't take either the warning or the gift seriously. It wasn't any more than two weeks later when Gary found himself back in court on yet another charge for car theft. At this point, the court sent Gary to the MacLaren Reform School for Boys. The MacLaren Reform School was a correctional facility located in Woodburn, Oregon. The boys residing in MacLaren were anywhere from age 13 to 25, and had committed and range of crimes. In retrospect, due to Gary's immense intelligence and his own willful nature, it might have been the fact that he was sent to MacLaren that had redoubled his affinity for crime, or at least his unwillingness to stop.

Gary was released the next year from MacLaren, but he didn't stay out for long. For the next several years, Gary would be in and out of prison for various crimes. In 1960, at 20 years old, Gary was convicted of another car theft. This time, he was sentenced to time in the Oregon State Correctional Institute. He served a minimal amount of time there, and was even released later in the year. It was around this time in 1961, that Gary's father, Frank Gilmore Sr., was diagnosed with lung cancer. It was terminal. Gary's tumultuous relationship with his father was coming to an end.

In 1962, Gary was once more arrested. This time, the crime was much more severe than stealing a car. He was charged with armed robbery and assault, and was sentenced to Oregon State Penitentiary. It was during this stint in prison that Frank Gilmore Sr. passed away from lung cancer. Gary was in prison at the time and was unable to say goodbye, or even receive the news directly from his family. One of the guards that the Oregon State Penitentiary gave Gary the news about his father's passing.

Gary's relationship with his father had never been good. He grew up in a household where his father and mother were always at odds, with him and his brother's caught in the middle. Frank Gilmore, Sr. was brutal, violent and strict on his sons. He went beyond disciplining them when he raised his belt or whip against Gary and his brothers. Mikal had even once described their father as a "cruel and unreasonable man". And yet, despite all of that - despite the years spent moving around at the whim of his con man father, and despite the years spent at the end of a leather strop and watching his father beat his mother, Gary Gilmore was distraught over the old man's death. When he was given the news of Frank Sr.'s passing, Gary tried to end his life by slitting his wrists.

The suicide attempt was unsuccessful, and Gary Gilmore remained alive. He was eventually released back into suicide. For two years, Gary either stayed out of trouble or managed not to get caught. And yet, in 1964, Gary was once more returned to prison - on the charges of armed robbery and assault, once more. This time, Gary was sentenced to fifteen years in prison for his habitual offenses. A prison psychiatrist finally diagnosed Gary with antisocial personality disorder as well as something called intermittent psychotic decompensation. Psychotic decompensation is a term that describes the rapid deterioration of someone's mental health that they had been, up until then, been otherwise maintaining. This, along with Gary's personality disorder characterized by his disregard and often violation of other people's rights and autonomy, make him a perfect package for crime.

By the time he was 30, Gary Gilmore had spent the greater part of his adult life in and out of prison. The intelligence that had heard him such high marks and a promising future when he was a boy didn't disappear over the years. In fact, Gary used much of his time in prison to write poetry and make artwork. It was these talents that initially won Gary conditional release to a halfway house in Eugene, Oregon. In 1972, he was granted permission to live weekdays at the halfway house under the condition that he stay out of trouble and take art classes at the local community college. However, in line with Gary's usual behavior, he ended up never registering for classes at the community college. Within a month of his initial conditional release, Gary Gilmore couldn't resist the siren call of crime, and was once more arrested and convicted on the charge of armed robbery.

Gary Gilmore's behavior in prison turned from quiet poetry crafting to violence, and he was eventually transferred to a maximum-security federal prison in Marion, Illinois. He was transferred there in 1975. Now 35, it was looking like Gary Gilmore would be spending many more years of is still short life in prison. While he was serving his time in Marion, Gary began writing letters with his cousin, Brenda Nicol. Perhaps it was through Gary's particular intelligence that he manipulated her into believing he deserved a second change, or maybe it was Brenda's own idea. All the same, in 1976, Gary was once more given conditional release into the care of his cousin, Brand. He would live with her in Provo, Utah, under the condition that he stay out of trouble. Brenda would help him look for work and aid in his reform, offering Gary a support system that he had not had previously.

Gary began working at a shoe repair store owned by his uncle, Vern Damico. He also worked, briefly, for an insulation company. This rehabilitation seemed to be on the up and up, and Gary's life was being steered clear of all his previous habits. Unfortunately, Gary wasn't able to keep away from his old ways for long. Soon after his foray into a new life, Gary was back into his old habits of drinking, stealing and fighting. He got into a relationship with a 19 year old woman by the name of Nicole Baker. Nicole was both a window and a divorcee and she had two young children at the time that she and Gary got together. Their relationship was casual at first, but it didn't take long for things between Gary and Nicole to become both intense and strained. Perhaps it was from his own parent's relationship that Gary had learned how to interact with others in a romantic sense - that is, he didn't learn very well at all.

Gary soon began imitate his father. He became controlling with Nicole, and threatening. Their relationship was strained both from Gary's violent behavior, as well as pressure from Nicole's family for her to leave him. Gary was having trouble adjusting to life outside of prison, after spending nearly half of his life, and almost all of his adult life, behind bars. His relationship with Nicole was just a precursor to Gary's inevitable inability to reform himself and stay the straight and narrow path.

It all came to a head on July 19th, 1976. Gary Gilmore stopped at a gas station in Orem, Utah. He had been travelling at the time with April, Nicole Baker's younger sister. During this time, Gary and Nicole were still off-again on-again, in an unstable and volatile relationship. It was around 10:30 in the evening that Gary stopped and told April that he needed to make a phone call. He left April in the car and entered the gas station. It was there that he robbed the gas station attendant, Max Jensen, at gunpoint, continuing his affinity for armed robbery. This time, however, Gary took it another step. After Gary had instructed Jensen to give him the money box, he forced him into the bathroom and had him lay down on the floor. Max Jensen obeyed all of Gary's demands, but his obedience was for naught. According to Gary's confession of the crime, he held his gun against Jensen's head and said, "This one is for me," before firing the gun once. He then stated, "For Nicole", before firing the gun a second time, shooting Jensen twice and then leaving him, dead and bleeding, on the bathroom floor of the gas station.

Leaving Orem behind, Gary traveled back to Provo with April and spent the night in a motel nearby where he left his truck in a service garage to be repaired. The evening after his armed robbery and murder in Orem, Gary robbed a hotel manager by the name of Ben Bushnell, who lived on the property with his family. Much like the victim before him, Ben Bushnell complied with every one of Gary's demands. An eyewitness, motel guest Peter Arroyo, would later describe Gary ordering Bushnell to lie on the floor. Much like Jensen, Bushnell was shot and killed. When he tried to dispose of his weapon that he used in both robberies and murders, Gary managed to accidentally shoot himself in his right hand. Had he not, he might have managed to get away with both killings and continue on to commit more escalated violence. As it were, his bleeding hand alerted the garage mechanic, Michael Simpson, who had seen Gary trying to hide the gun in the nearby bushes.

Michael Simpson wrote down Gary's license plate number after hearing about a shooting at a nearby motel on a police scanner. He called the police and alerted them of the goings on, of Gary's wounded hand and of his disposing of the gun in the bushes by the mechanic garage. Meanwhile, Gary had called his cousin for support, but she was unsympathetic to his plight. She called the police as well, and Gary was taken into custody after law enforcement found him at the edge of town not long after the incident.

Gary Mark Gilmore isn't the most prolific killer in history, or even of his time. He probably wouldn't even be classified as a serial killer, or even a spree killer. It's Gary's particular circumstances that make him so famous, however. It was the same year that Gary Mark Gilmore was arrested for two counts of murder that the U.S Supreme Court upheld a series of new death penalty statutes in the court decision of Gregg v. Georgia. Before that, death penalty statutes had been deemed "cruel and unusual punishment", and therefore deemed unconstitutional. It wasn't until the 1976 Supreme Court decision that the death penalty was reinstated. Perhaps, if this ruling had not occurred, Gary Mark Gilmore would have rotted away in life in prison as many others had before him during the time where the death penalty was not in effect. Gary Mark Gilmore was charged with both the murders of Jensen and Bushnell, though only Bushnell's murder actually went to trial, due to a lack of evidence and eyewitnesses to Jensen's murder—even though Gary admitted to both.

He was held in custody until October 5th, 1976. It was on that day that Gary Mark Gilmore's trail began in Provo. It lasted only two days. Unhappy with his lawyers' lack of cross-examination and lack of their own witnesses for his defense, Gary persuaded the judge to let him take the stand in his own defense. He claimed dissociation and lack of control, and tried to make a case of insanity. His own attorney's called four separate psychiatrists to shoot down this attempt of claiming insanity, showing that Gary had full control and awareness of what he was doing during the crimes. Not even his antisocial personality disorder was enough for him to actually meet the legal definition of insanity. Despite his intelligence and his skilled manipulation tactics, Gary was not able to present a defense for himself. It seemed that he knew when he was beat.

On October 7, 1976, after two days of trial, the jury returned a guilty verdict. They also agreed on the death penalty, due to circumstances surrounding Gary's crimes. This would be the first execution in the United States in ten years, and the first execution that would happen after the Supreme Court decision to allow the death penalty once more.

Gary's mother, Bessie, attempted to sue to for a stay of execution, despite the fact that Gary himself chose not to pursue habeas corpus. In a unanimous decision, the U.S Supreme Court refused to even hear Bessie's claim, and her son was slated to be executed. A death penalty sentence in modern times includes lethal injection, as it has been proven to be the most humane way of sentencing a criminal to death, unlike the methods of the past such as hanging or the electric chair. During Utah in 1976, however, the only methods available for executions were hanging, or a firing squad. Gary Mark Gilmore had already accepted his fate as the first man to be executed in the United States in almost ten years. To Gary, a hanging had room for error. He told the court, "I prefer to be shot," and chose the firing squad. Thus, his execution was set for 8 am on November 15th.

Despite having accepted his fate, Gary ended up actually receiving a few stays of execution, though he did not seek them out and explicitly did not want them. It was at the hands of the American Civil Liberties Union (ACLU) and his attorneys that drew out his already chosen execution. When his lawyers tried to call of an appeal on his case, Gary opted instead to fire them. He was ready to face his death, and he saw no reason to draw it out any longer. It was this refusal of appeal that drew the ACLU's attention. The ACLU made efforts, hand in hand with the National Association for the Advancement of Colored People to turn over Gary's execution. However, it wasn't entirely for Gary's benefit. They were using Gary's case to benefit the prisoners who were standing on death row throughout the United States, all of whom were now in danger of facing execution now that the Supreme Court had reinstated the death penalty.

Gary's execution got tied up in legalities. He was ready for it to all be over. In November 1976, while Gary was taking part in a Board of Pardons hearing, Gary said this of all the legal attempts to spare his life: "It's been sanctioned by the courts that I die and I accept that." The dragged out legal battle between the courts and the ACLU put off Gary's execution for months, and in the interim Gary attempted suicide twice. His first attempted occurred on November 16th when his first stay of execution was announced. Nicole Barrett visited Gary in prison, despite her having broken off their relationship. They kissed and held one another during Nicole's visit, and the reason for it became clear. Nicole had snuck in sleeping pills. After she had left, Gary swallowed the overdose of pills—while at the same time, miles away in her own home, Nicole Barrett had done the same, the both of them attempting suicide. Gary had not taken enough sleeping pills for the dosage to be fatal. Nicole took a larger dosage of sleeping pills, which resulted in her slipping into a coma for several days. Gary was not finished with attempting to end his life. With or without Nicole, Gary attempted suicide again one month later to the exact day in December. When that didn't work, he took up a hunger strike.

Finally, Gary was given a date for execution: January 17th, 1977. On the night before his execution, Gary requested that he be allowed to have an all-night gathering that consisted of his friends and family. He was granted the request, and spent his last evening surrounded by the people in his life that could be considered his loved ones. Gary's last meal consisted of potatoes and steak to eat, and milk and coffee to drink. For whatever reason, Gary didn't touch his steak and potatoes. The last thing that he had was the milk and the coffee. The next morning, on January 17th, Gary's last stay of execution was overturned at 7:30 AM, and Gary was finally allowed to go through with his execution as he had wanted so many months previously.

At 8:07 AM, Gary was taken behind the prison to an abandoned cannery. He was placed and secured into a chair with a wall of sandbags behind him for the purpose of absorbing the bullets. In tradition of firing squad, five local police were placed behind a cloth with only a small hole for them to put through the barrel of their rifles, aimed directly at his body from 20 feet away. In Utah tradition, the firing squad consists of four men with live rounds and one man with a blank round. This is done, ostensibly, so that the men comprised of the firing squad will never know which one of them fired the killing shot.

When he was asked for any last words, all Gary Mark Gilmore had to say was this: "Let's do it!" A black hood was placed on his head, and the five gunmen were allowed to fire a single bullet into the body of the first man to undergo execution in the United States in almost ten years.

Gary's youngest brother, Mikal Gilmore, was allowed to inspect the clothes worn by his brother after his execution. Allegedly, there were five holes left in the clothes, not four. He noted this in his memoir, 'Shot in the Heart', and mused that Utah wanted to take no chances on leaving his brother alive. Mikal's memoir goes in depth into his relationship with Gary, as well as the strained relationship he had with his family, as well as the aftermath of his own brother's execution at the hands of the state of Utah.

Before his death, Gary had requested that his organs be donated to those in need of transplant. Because of his death by firing squad, it can be presumed that some of his internal organs were useless, now riddled with bullet holes - mainly, his heart, where a piece of black cloth had been pinned as a target for the firing squad. Strangely enough, though, two people were able to receive corneal transplants, courtesy of now famed murderer Gary Mark Gilmore. After his autopsy, Gary's body was cremated. In a grandiose decision by his family, Gary's ashes were then scattered from an airplane over Spanish Fork, Utah.

Gary Mark Gilmore is notorious, perhaps not for his crimes, but for when his crimes occurred. He would have otherwise rotted away in prison, unknown but for the people whose lives he had touched, no matter how horrid and terrible that touch may be. It was by virtue of the place and time that he had committed his crimes that gained Gary Mark Gilmore his fame of being the first man executed in the United States since the death penalty had been reinstated. It is more than just those who were involved in his case and legal battles that remember his name. Gary Mark Gilmore is now known for his own battle for execution. He is remembered in both the minds of those involved, as well as the legal histories of the United States.

www.ingramcontent.com/pod-product-compliance
Lightning Source LLC
Chambersburg PA
CBHW022009120726
47992CB00001B/489